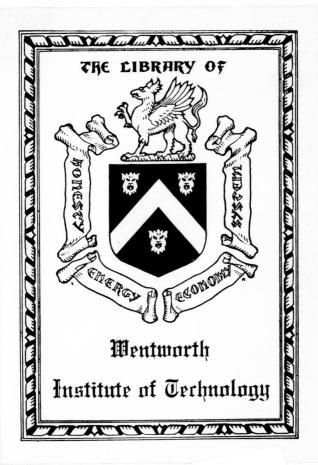

In the same series

The Critical Idi

Founder Editor: John D. Jump 1969 - 1

41 The Balla

The Ballad/*Alan Bold*

Methuen & Co Ltd

First published in 1979 by
Methuen & Co. Ltd
11 New Fetter Lane, London EC4P 4EE

Published in the USA by
Methuen & Co. Ltd
a division of Methuen, Inc.
733 Third Avenue, New York, NY 10017

Typeset by Inforum Ltd, Portsmouth
Printed in Great Britain by
J. W. Arrowsmith Ltd, Bristol

ISBN 0 416 70890 0 (hardback edition)
ISBN 0 416 70900 1 (paperback edition)

Contents

1
Origin of the ballads

I have often been afraid of dying before 1879 ended. I want to
live long enough to put the world in possession of all the English
ballads, and find it frequently necessary to say to myself that this
is the only matter of essential importance.
                              (Francis James Child, letter of 24 January
                                        1880 to Sven Grundtvig)

What is a ballad? It is one of the minor tragedies of literature
that the man best equipped to answer that question did not live
to do so. Professor Francis James Child, whose five-volume
epic of scholarship *The English and Scottish Popular Ballads*
(1882-98) contains the definitive ballad canon, died in Boston
on 11 September 1896 at the age of seventy-one. He had spent
the greatest years of his scholastic life collecting material for
his monumental anthology and at his death he had completed
the work — with the significant omission of his proposed General
Introduction. Among Child's papers were the beginnings
of the draft of the Introduction:

> In the moderate compass of less than five vol[ume]s there
> has now been gathered everything in the Eng[lish] language
> that by the most liberal interpretation could be called a pop-
> ular ballad, and all the known versions of such.
> (Child MSS, Harvard Library, Vol. XVI, p. 132)

What Child had done was to collect and annotate 305 ballads
with around 1000 versions. His claims to completeness were
sound. Since his death, avid collectors have tried to add to the
Child canon — with items like 'Still Growing', 'Corpus

Christi', 'Bruton Town' — but only one piece has been accepted everywhere as a genuine popular ballad: 'The Bitter Withy', which Frank Sidgwick contributed to *Notes and Queries,* 29 July 1905.

A fastidious scholar, Child chose his words with care. The definite article in his title is a deliberate assertion of finality; the epithet 'popular' contains the key to the whole collection. Child was interested only in ballads that were produced or possessed by the people: broadside ballads were, he felt, a low form of artistic composition, though he reluctantly used broadside texts of popular ballads; ballad imitations he found absurd. The popular ballad was an oral phenomenon, a narrative song that had been preserved on the lips of unlettered people. His editorial method followed the principles of Sven Grundtvig whose great *Danmarks gamle Folkeviser* (the first volume of which was published in Copenhagen in 1853) assembled the Danish ballads. Like Grundtvig, Child ascribed a number to each ballad and a letter to each version of that ballad; all the popular ballads cited in this book are classified according to the Child code. Hence the first item in Child's collection is 'Riddles Wisely Expounded' (1A) while the final item is 'The Outlaw Murray' (305C). Quotations from Child on any particular ballad are excerpted from his headnotes to that ballad.

The modern reader has lived so long with ballads as a permanent feature of every library that it requires an imaginative leap to conceive of a time when the ballads had no fixed texts and were simply and fondly remembered by those who enjoyed singing them. Critics have constructed such a massive academic apparatus around these beautiful songs that there are times when the direct power of the ballads is obscured. When topics like modality and musical morphology are being debated, it is salutary to remember that many of the songs under critical scrutiny were sung, not by sophisticated musical performers, but by milkmaids and nurses and ploughmen. When the structural minutia of the ballads is being clinically dissected it is essential to recall that actual ballads preceded the impressive theories and not vice versa. In other words the ideal approach to the ballads is first to let them speak for themselves and only then to arrive at schemata which make a total grasp of the subject possible. It is arguable that the commentators on balladry have — through their collective critical efforts — overshadowed, not illuminated, the brilliance of the original product.

When the ballads floated around in the oral atmosphere inhaled by non-literate but naturally gifted folk, they were ignored by historians and literary critics. When they began to be dragged from this natural environment there was an unnatural curiosity as to the origins of this particular species of singing poetry. The style was so obviously finished and perfected that the speculators got to work with their obfuscatory powers. Ballad theorists have been quick to rush in where common sense fears to tread, and an acrimonious debate has arisen over the beginnings of balladry. In Germany Johann Gottfried von Herder (1744-1803), committed to a national renaissance, insisted on the spontaneous folk origin of ballads. The *Volkslieder* (or, as he preferred, *Nationallieder)* were expressions of the pure voice of the people.

Once upon a time, too, there was Jakob Grimm (1785-1863) — whose picture hung in Child's study — and he held that popular poetry and fairy tales were collectively composed by the folk: *das Volk dichtet.* This notion that the folk make the poetry has come to be known as the communalist theory. We are asked to believe that a primitive community spontaneously made poetry together, much as they might cooperate to make a fire. Outside Germany this conjecture became a matter of dogmatic literary warfare. Francis B. Gummere's books took the communalist premiss to a fanciful conclusion. He postulated the existence of a primitive throng concentrating their attention on an event of local significance and making a marvellous song and dance out of it. In his introduction to his one-volume reduction of Child, George L. Kittredge positively embraced the notion:

> Different members of the throng, one after another, may chant his verse, composed on the spur of the moment, and the sum of these various contributions makes a song. This is communal composition, though each verse, taken by itself, is the work of an individual. A song made in this way is no man's property and has no individual author. *The folk is its author*, ... the history of balladry, if we could follow it back in a straight line without interruptions, would lead us to very simple conditions of society, to the singing and dancing throng, to a period of communal composition.
>
> (*English and Scottish Popular Ballads,* pp. xix and xxii)

It is significant that neither Gummere nor Kittredge could claim that any extant ballad was produced in this way. Their speculations were confined to an archetypal ballad; their theories were based on illuminations received inside the library. Neither of them had any experience of primitive societies; neither of them had any personal insight into the creative process. They were basically stating what they felt ought to be the case, for it was imperative, they believed, to explain away the ballad phenomenon. Cecil Sharp, on the other hand, when he published *English Folk Song: Some Conclusions* in 1907, had spent some four years collecting some 1 500 folksongs (mainly from Somerset) and his opinions had the benefit of first-hand experience in the field. Sharp realized that any ballad must first be the work of an individual but that the community had an important secondary role to play. His statement is probably the most lucid and compelling summary of the communalist-individualist debate:

> Every line, every word of [a] ballad sprang in the first instance from the head of some individual, reciter, minstrel, or peasant; just as every note, every phrase of a folk tune proceeded originally from the mouth of a solitary singer. Cor-

porate action has originated nothing and can originate nothing. Communal composition is unthinkable. The community plays a part, it is true, but it is at a later stage, after and not before the individual has done his work and manufactured the material. Its part is then to weigh, sift, and select from the mass of individual suggestions those which most accurately express the popular taste and the popular ideal; to reject the rest; and then, when more variations are produced, to repeat the process once more, and again once more. The process goes on unceasingly while the ballad lives; or until it gets into print when, of course, its process is checked, so far as educated singers are concerned.

(English Folk Song: Some Conclusions, p. 41)

So — the individual is creative, the performer is re-creative, the folk are a selective audience. Sharp, who initiated the folksong revival in England and reminded the critics that a ballad is not a ballad unless it has a tune, ended much confusion with that statement.

Once we have accepted the individual composition and subsequent folk possession of a ballad, there is the question of the antiquity of the phenomenon. 'Judas' (13), which exists in a thirteenth-century manuscript, is the oldest English ballad preserved in writing. However, as the whole weight of scholarship has supported the oral nature of balladry, the existence of manuscripts or printed texts is not conclusive. A ballad may have been orally transmitted for years before being written down or printed. We can only say that the ballad seems to be a medieval invention which had oral currency up to the eighteenth century, when the collectors began to preserve these popular treasures. Then, as Edwin Muir put it in his 'Complaint of the Dying Peasantry':

> The singing and the harping fled
> Into the silent library.

By the nineteenth century new popular ballads had ceased to

be composed orally, though variants of ballad stories proliferated. By then the folk had been industrialized, mass literacy had been introduced, and primary oral composition was a thing of the past. The folk did not lose their creative impetus; they simply transferred it to the printed word.

It was the literary men who made the ballad a prestigious enough article to be granted the status of hard covers in the course of time. It was a slow process. Eminent Elizabethans like Shakespeare (see Autolycus in *The Winter's Tale*) and Jonson (see Nightingale in *Bartholomew Fair*) had no high opinion of ballads or ballad-mongers. Then Sir Philip Sidney, in his *Apologie for Poetrie* (1595), expressed his enthusiasm, albeit apologetically, for 'The Hunting of the Cheviot' (162A):

> Certainly I must confess my own barbarousness. I never heard the olde song of Percy and Duglas that I found not my heart mooved more then with a trumpet; and yet it is sung but by some blinde crouder, with no rougher voyce then rude stile: which, being so evill apparrelled in the dust and cobwebbes of that uncivill age, what would it worke trymmed in the gorgeous eloquence of Pindar!

That was the first influential tribute to the emotional power of the ballads. The growing awareness of the ballads, particularly 'Chevy Chase' (162B) which is a broadside version of 'The Hunting of the Cheviot' (162A), among the literati is attested in Matthew Prior's 'Satyr on the Poets' (1687) where he says:

> By Verse you'l starve; *John Saul* cou'd never live,
> Unless the Bell-Man made the Poet thrive:
> Go rather, in some little Shed by *Pauls,*
> Sell *Chivy Chase,* and *Baxter's* Salve for Souls.

Here we have the contrast between the isolated art-poet and the mass appeal of the ballads.

It was in the heyday of neoclassicism that the ballads found their first real champion. In 1711 — the year of Pope's *Essay on Criticism* — Joseph Addison, arbiter of taste, devoted two

Spectator papers (Nos 70 and 74) to a discussion of 'Chevy Chase' (162B) and a further paper (No. 85) to 'The Two Children in the Wood', 'one of the darling songs of the common people'. Addison argued that 'an Heroic poem should be founded upon some important precept of Morality'. This principle, which undeniably applied to Homer's *Iliad* and Virgil's *Aeneid,* was also seen in 'Chevy Chase' (162B) which, Addison reminded readers of the *Spectator,* was 'the favourite Ballad of the people of England'. Addison compared the death of Turnus in the *Aeneid* with the death of Earl Douglas:

> Who never sayd more words than these:
>> Fight on, my merry men all!
> For why, my life is att an end,
>> Lord Pearcy sees my fall.

Convinced a poem should be distinguished by stylistic and thematic clarity, Addison argued that the nobility of 'Chevy Chase' (162B) was a matter of 'majestic simplicity'. The ballad's classical power was more rewarding than the pretentious artifice of 'gothic' (i.e. Metaphysical) poetry. Far from despising the popularity of the ballad, Addison saw this as evidence of its quality, for it had stood the test of time and repeated hearings: 'an ordinary song or ballad, that is the delight of the common people, cannot fail to please all such readers as are not unqualified for the entertainment by their affectation or ignorance . . .' Although Addison's eulogy on 'Chevy Chase' (162B) was held to be an intellectual aberration by such critics as John Dennis, the fact that a brilliant man of letters had endorsed the ballad had vast repercussions. Addison had isolated the quality of simplicity and this would determine much of the subsequent appreciation of the ballads. A neat couplet from Dr John Armstrong's *Taste: An Epistle to a Young Critic* (1753) facetiously acknowledged the shift in sensibility caused by Addison:

> But thanks to Heav'n and Addison's good grace
> Now ev'ry fop is charm'd with Chevy Chase.

A scholar who was decidedly charmed by Addison's arguments was Thomas Percy (1721-1811), Bishop of Dromore from 1782. Although he has often been vilified for his dubious editorial methods, Percy remains the man who instigated the modern interest in ballads and, with it, the Romantic revival. The picturesque story of Percy's discovery of a seventeenth-century folio has a nice symbolic touch. Percy found some maids using sheets from the manuscript to light fires; as he explained in a note inside the cover of his folio:

> This very curious Old Manuscript in its present mutilated state, but unbound and sadly torn, &c . . . I rescued from destruction, and begged at the hands of my worthy friend Humphrey Pitt Esq., then living at Shiffnal in Shropshire . . . I saw it lying dirty on the floor under a Bureau in ye Parlour: being used by the Maids to light the fire.
>
> (J.W. Hales and F.J. Furnivall, (eds), *Bishop Percy's Folio Manuscript,* Vol. I, p. lxiv)

Percy rescued the manuscript from the flames, and his use of it set fire to the European imagination. The folio manuscript, dated *c.* 1650, contained 191 lyrical and narrative poems and Percy decided to use it as the basis of an anthology of ballads. On the advice of his friend, the poet Shenstone, Percy altered many of the texts in an attempt to make the collection more palatable to the taste of the eighteenth-century public. Nor was his planned publication a printed version of the folio manuscript; for when that was re-edited (with the forceful backing of Child) by J. W. Hales and F. J. Furnivall in 1867 it transpired that only about one in four of Percy's reliques came from his original source. Percy extended his field by inspecting broadside collections, such as the one made by Samuel Pepys, and by relying on correspondents like Sir David Dalrymple (Lord Hailes), who contributed 'Edward' (13B) and 'Sir Patrick Spens' (58A).

The first edition of Percy's *Reliques of Ancient English*

Poetry, containing 176 items, was published in February 1765 (subsequent editions appeared in 1767, 1775 and 1794). In an introduction Percy took up Addison's point about simplicity and emotional grandeur:

> In a polished age, like the present, I am sensible that many of these reliques of antiquity will require great allowances to be made for them. Yet have they, for the most part, a pleasing simplicity, and many artless graces, which in the opinion of no mean critics [Percy's footnote identifies 'Mr Addison, Mr Dryden and the witty Lord Dorset'] have been thought to compensate for the want of higher beauties, and, if they do not dazzle the imagination, are frequently found to interest the heart.

Percy's book is one of the most influential in English literature. It was a novel presentation of old songs and thus combined antiquarian interests with advanced opinion. There was something there for everyone. On impressionable poetic minds the *Reliques* descended with explosive force. Sir Walter Scott, in his brief Autobiography (included in Lockhart's *Life*), remembered how Percy altered his thirteen-year-old consciousness:

> To read and remember was in this instance the same thing, and henceforth I overwhelmed my school-fellows, and all who would hearken to me, with tragic recitations from the Ballads of Bishop Percy. The first time, too, I could scrape a few shillings together ... I bought unto myself a copy of these beloved volumes; nor do I believe I ever read a book half so frequently, or with half the enthusiasm.

Percy included in his book a glowing portrait of the medieval minstrelsy. We now distinguish between popular ballads (those orally composed by amateurs) and minstrel ballads (those composed by professionals) but Percy thought all his ballads were produced by minstrels, fine fellows who were welcomed at the homes of the rich and powerful. These romantic characters, with their harps and ready eloquence, became part of the general literary imagination. Scott accepted Percy's account of the minstrels, called his own great ballad collection *Minstrelsy of the Scottish Border,* and wrote 'The Lay of the Last Minstrel'.

Now the minstrel ballads are conspicuously different from the popular ballads. Whereas the popular ballads are impersonal, the minstrel ballads draw attention to the presence of the narrator who usually tells his audience to 'Lyth and listen'. Whereas the folk ballads do not specify settings, the minstrel ballads dwell on topographical details. Whereas the traditional ballads rush into the narrative heart of the matter, the minstrel ballads display a leisurely approach to the story. A fine minstrel ballad, 'Robin Hood and the Monk' (119) — which exists in a manuscript dated *c.* 1450 — opens with a grand atmospheric flourish:

> In somer, when the shawes be sheyne,
> And leves be large and long,
> Hit is full mery in feyre forests
> To here the foulys song:

> To se the dere draw to the dale,
> And leve the hilles hee,
> And shadow hem in the leves grene,
> Under the grene-wode tre.

The Robin Hood sequence, which includes some excellent poems, was accepted by Child because he felt the minstrels had reworked a popular tradition. However, the minstrel was a professional entertainer, not a folksinger.

This distinction was crucial to Joseph Ritson (1752-1803), a formidable scholar who produced a mass of editorial work including *Pieces of Ancient Popular Poetry* (1791), *Scottish Song* (1794) and *Robin Hood* (1795). Unfortunately Ritson was of a rather unstable temperament, inclined to verbal and, latterly, physical violence. He began as a vegetarian and idola-

tor of Mary Queen of Scots and ended up insane and impecuni-
ous. He rejected Percy's portrayal of the minstrel as far-fetched
and argued instead that the minstrel was an ill-educated itiner-
ant who amused the lowly at fairs and at roadsides. Facts
about minstrels are few and far between. In 'The Battle of Otterburn' (161A) Harry Percy calls on both his archers and his minstrels:

> Wherefore schote, archars, for my sake,
>   And let scharpe arowes flee;
> Mynstrells, plays up for your waryson [reward],
>   And well quyt it schall bee.

However, a different picture is given in George Puttenham's
treatise on *The Arte of English Poesie* (1589) where we meet

> ... taverne minstrels that give a fit of mirth for a groat, &
> their matters being for the most part stories of old time, as
> the tale of Sir *Topas,* the reportes of *Beuis* of *Southampton,*
> *Guy* of *Warwicke, Adam Bell* and *Clymme of the Clough* &
> such other old Romances or historicall rimes, made pur-
> posely for recreation of the common people at Christmasse
> diners & brideales, and in tavernes & alehouses and such
> other places of base resort, also they be used in Carols and
> rounds and such light or lascivious Poemes, which are com-
> monly more commodiously uttered by these buffons or
> vices in playes then by any other person.

In MS Ashmole 48 'The Hunting of the Cheviot' (162A) is sub-
scribed 'Expliceth, quod Richard Sheale', but Child denied
that this signified authorship: 'This ballad was of course part of
his stock as minstrel; the supposition that he was the author is
preposterous in the extreme.'

Apart from his determination to reverse Percy's picture of
the minstrel, Ritson was extremely sceptical of the authenticity
of Percy's folio manuscript and challenged him to produce it so
a comparison could be made with the printed *Reliques.* Percy's

refusal to do so infuriated Ritson, and he was even more out-
raged at the blatantly fraudulent collections of *Scottish Tragic
Ballads* (1781) and *Select Scottish ballads* (1783) produced by
John Pinkerton. Ritson himself was a scrupulously exact editor of texts and, when he could, he printed music for the ballads. He can thus be regarded — in his method, not his
madness — as the model of the modern ballad scholar who
insists on untampered texts and on matching text and tune.

Until the time of Child the ballad men found themselves in
either the Percy or the Ritson camp: that is, they either
'improved' received ballads or printed them verbatim. Sir Walter Scott, in his *Minstrelsy* (1802-3), emulated Percy's
approach; William Motherwell's *Minstrelsy Ancient and Modern* (1827) adhered to Ritsonian standards of accuracy. Scott
was so skilful at amending his texts that it is still difficult to
ascertain how much of 'Kinmont Willie' (186) is traditional
and how much the poet's own work. Scott came to regret his
attitude, for in a letter of 3 May 1825 to Motherwell he con-
fessed: 'I think I did wrong myself in endeavouring to make the
best possible set of an ancient ballad out of several copies
obtained from different quarters, and that in many respects if I
improved the poetry I spoiled the simplicity of the old song.'
The tide had turned in Ritson's favour and it was left to Child
to gather in the oceanic riches of traditional balladry.

Thanks to modern scholarship (see especially Friedman's
The Ballad Revival) we know how the word 'ballad' became
current in the English language. The term is derived from the
French *ballade* (which in turn comes from the Latin *ballare,* to
dance). The French ballads conformed to a strict pattern —
three stanzas, linked by a refrain, rhyming ababbcbC (C being
the refrain). When the idiom was imported to England in the fifteenth century the interstanzaic rhyming was dropped (English
being more barren in rhymes than French), as was the restric-
tion on length. Thus the English ballade 'London Lickpenny'
(dating from the second half of the fifteenth century) com-

prises sixteen stanzas. Apart from the refrain and the sixth line
that is matched to it, there is no rhyme common to the whole
poem, yet each stanza adheres to the ababbcbc format:

> In to London I gan me to hy
> of all the lond it bearethe the prise
> hot pescods, one can cry
> strabery rype, and chery in the ryse
> one bad me come nere and by some spice
> pepar and saffron they gan me bede
> clove, grayns, and flowre of Rise
> for lacke of money I might not spede

The English ballade was normally political, or tropical or
satirical (like 'London Lickpenny'); as such it was issued in
the broadside format. Skelton's elegy on King Henry VII (*c.*
1509), probably the oldest printed broadside ballad, is written
in seven ballad stanzas. Eventually all broadside poems were
referred to as ballads, and when the traditional narrative songs
of the people came to be printed as broadsides they too were
called ballads and the name stuck (with disastrous terminologi-
cal consequences, for to this day the word 'ballad' is so vague
that it can be used for a broadside or a traditional narrative
song or a slow piece of popular music). Ironically, then, the traditional ballad takes its name from the despised broadside that
is held to be so inferior to it.

Admittedly the qualitative difference between popular and
broadside ballads is immense. The broadsides were urban arte-
facts that aimed at permanence and proved ephemeral; the popular ballads were produced for the folk and possessed by them.
Mrs Hogg, the mother of the Ettrick Shepherd, provided Sir
Walter Scott with invaluable material and later told him that
print had a destructive effect on the ballads:

There war never ane o' my sangs prentit till ye prentit them
yoursel', an' ye hae spoilt them awthegither. They were
made for singing an' no for reading; but ye hae broken the

charm now, an' they'll never be sung mair.

(James Hogg, *Domestic Manners
of Sir Walter Scott* (1834), p. 61)

They were made for singing: that is the modern conception of
the popular ballad. It is a narrative song whose metrical structure conforms to the exigencies of memorability. Because the
popular ballads had an oral currency they had to be memorable, and all the stylistic features we associate with balladry
can be explained by the fact that to survive they had to be unfor-
gettable. The simple rhymes, the incremental reputations, the
obligatory epithets, the magical numbers, the nuncupative tes-
taments, the commonplace phrases, the reliance on dialogue,
the dramatic nature of the narrative: these make the ballad
easier to remember, easier to memorize. The unique style of the
ballads derives from its oral nature. Literary poetry, written
for the page, depends on the unexpected phrase, the ingenious
rhyme, the contrived figure of speech. Literary poets like to
innovate; oral poets must depend on formulas.

Those ballads at the beginning of Child's collection have a
large number of Continental analogues, and it was surely in
response to a European stock of stories that the English and
Scottish ballads first evolved their unmistakable style. What
we call the ballad style was the simplest mould into which to
pour these stories. Once fitted to the basic ballad shape they
could travel and assume local characteristics; the story,
though, remained fairly constant. Once the ballad style had
been fixed as a convenient mental package for storing narratives, the way was clear for indigenous ballads — hence the
Robin Hood sequence in England and the Border sequence in
Scotland.

An unlettered person had to rely on conventions and a con-
temptably familiar structure in order to retain a large number
of stories. The evolution of the form made memorization
easier, made it possible for the mind to lock on to a definite con-

ceptual shape. It was this shape that was fixed in the brain, and when it passed from mind to mind, via the oral tradition, incidental variations were inevitable. Having learned the overall shape the ballad singer would alter it in singing, and when new singers absorbed the shape they would adapt it according to time and place and circumstance. There are thus dozens of variants of particular ballad stories and this is why Child, as a scholar, printed all the extant versions instead of adopting Scott's practice of collating one text. Even when popular ballads were issued as broadsides, they were often returned to the oral tradition and altered all over again.

So ballads are schematic story-containers sturdy enough to retain their basic shape despite repeated usage by different people. Child printed twenty-two versions of 'Lamkin' (93) but all of them tell the same tale. Each singer's individuality was conditioned by the requirements of the story. Each performance permitted an element of improvization but that was limited to details. The story was the stable element. The most celebrated ballad singer was Mrs Brown of Falkland who learned ballads from the singing of three women — her mother, her nurse and her aunt Anne Farquharson. In a letter of 21 April 1800 to Alexander Fraser Tytler she explained the oral nature of her ballad stock: 'they are written down entirely from recollection, for I never saw one of them in print or manuscript; but I learned them all when a child, by hearing them sung ... '

We know that Mrs Brown re-created the ballads when she performed them on the evidence of her two versions of 'The Lass of Roch Royal' (76). The first version was performed in 1783 when she was thirty-six; the second in 1800 when she was fifty-three. Both versions tell the same story — of how Annie of Roch Royal sails the sea to be reunited with Love Gregor, the father of her child; how Love Gregor's false mother bars the door to her by a cruel impersonation; how Annie then goes suicidally to a watery grave. 'The Lass of Roch Royal' (76D) comprises thirty-two quatrains while the later version (76E) has

twenty-eight. The early version identifies the dissimulation of
Love Gregor's mother immediately while the 1800 version contains an element of surprise.

The creative act of recomposition-in-performance can be
observed in the differences between functionally related stanzas. At the catastrophic moment the 1783 version has

> The wind grew loud, an the sea grew rough,
>> An the ship was rent in twain,
> An soon he saw her Fair Anny
>> Come floating oer the main.

> He saw his young son in her arms,
>> Baith tossd aboon the tide;
> He wrang his hands, then fast he ran,
>> An plung'd i the sea sae wide.

while the 1800 version has

> The wind blew loud, the sea grew rough,
>> And dashd the boat on shore;
> Fair Annie floats on the raging sea,
>> But her young son raise no more.

> Love Gregor tare his yellow hair,
>> And made a heavy moan;
> Fair Annie's corpse lay at his feet,
>> But his bonny young son was gone.

Discussing the differences between the two versions, Bronson
(*The Ballad as Song*, p. 71) commented that what Mrs Brown
retained was 'Not a *text*, but a *ballad*: a fluid entity soluble in
the mind, to be concretely realized at will in words and music.'
The same ability to re-create with each performance was noted
by Cecil Sharp:

> Mr Henry Larcombe, the blind singer ... will habitually
> vary every phrase of his tune in the course of a ballad. I
> remember that in the first song that he sang to me he varied

the first phrase of the second verse. I asked him to repeat the
verse that I might note the variation. He at once gave me a
third form of the same phrase.

(*English Folk Song: Some Conclusions,* pp. 28-9)

The number of variants shows that the ballads were not
only orally transmitted but orally *transmuted* as well. Secure
in the stable shape of their ballad story, the best singers could
admit variations. They could retouch the stylistic microstruc-
ture while respecting the narrative macrostructure. This process is somewhat mysterious to the modern mind because we
live in a literate society. Perhaps, though, the situation may be
illuminated by citing the one vital oral form that remains in our
culture — the common joke. How particular jokes originate
nobody but the originator knows (and he's not saying). If jokes
are good enough they pass into oral circulation and travel by
word of mouth. Yet the expert joke-teller never reproduces a
joke exactly: he retains the essential comic narrative but varies
the details to suit his mood, his environment, his audience. In
much the same way the ballads were transmitted (and — who
knows? — perhaps a Child will come along some day and store
the jokes in a vast five-volume thesaurus). As Motherwell
reminds us (*Minstrelsy Ancient and Modern*, p. iii), Chaucer's
Pardoner made the immortal observation:

> — Lewd peple loven tales olde;
> Swiche things can they wel report and holde.

Notwithstanding the aptness of that remark, it is a mis-
take to think of all the ballad folk as lewd or common folk.
Again the case of Mrs Brown of Falkland is instructive. She
was born Anna Gordon (1747-1810) in Aberdeen where her
father Thomas was Professor of Humanity at King's College.
She later married the Rev. Andrew Brown, minister at Falkland. Child said in his Advertisement to the first part of his collection that 'No Scottish ballads are superior in kind to those
recited in the last century by Mrs Brown, of Falkland'. She pre-

served thirty-three ballads, with variations, and all of them were canonized by Child, who made twenty of them A texts and four of them B texts. Nobody could be further from the communalist's notion of the dancing, singing peasant than Mrs Brown. The significant fact was that she lived in an age when there was an interaction between popular tradition and high culture. To this day, in Scotland, the expression 'folk' connotes simply the mass of the people. It has no mystical overtones. The eighteenth century, which has many claims to be the Golden Age of Balladry, is full of examples of interpenetration between the rural and urban, the sophisticated and the self-taught. The vigorous vernacular muse of Robert Burns, a tenant-farmer, conquered the Edinburgh literati. And it was Sir David Dalrymple, Lord Hailes, a Scottish Lord of Session, who communicated 'Edward' (13B) and 'Sir Patrick Spens' (58A) to Percy. Divisive class differences existed of course; but in a ballad context when we think of the folk we will do well to remember all of the folk all of the time.

Since Child's death most of the criticism directed against him has concentrated on his lack of interest in the musical side of the ballads. In a way Child left his successors little to do in the textual sense but collect variants of his 305 ballads. This they have done. However, the greatest contribution to a repossession of balladry has come from research into ballad music. It is true that Child was a literary scholar who was not really interested in ballad music; at the end of his collection he printed fifty-five tunes collected for him by his friend William Walker of Aberdeen. Child's pre-eminence as a collector was nevertheless due to his ear for the sound of the genuine popular ballad, and in a letter of 25 August 1872 to Sven Grundtvig he said: 'It is a pity one can't constantly insist on the lyrical, or singable, character [of the ballads] as a criterion.' The pioneering musical work on the ballads was done by Cecil Sharp who, before his death in 1924, had collected and hand-notated almost 5000 tunes and songs. A firm socialist, Sharp used the expression folksong 'exclusively to denote the song ... which has been created by the common people in contradistinction to the song ... which has been composed by the educated' *(English Folk Song: Some Conclusions.* p. 4). His evolutionary theory of folk music isolated three factors: *continuity,* which relies on the ability of the folk to remember and pass on songs; *variation,* which recognizes the ability of the folk to alter melodic lines; and *selection,* which acknowledges the ability of the folk to accept only those songs which appeal to them. In 1956 this continuity-variation-selection trinity was officially accepted as gospel by the International Folk Music Council.

The man who has done for ballad music what Child did for the words — that is, assembling and annotating all the material — is Bertrand Harris Bronson of the University of California in Berkeley. Basing his work principally on Cecil Sharp's collection of tunes, Bronson published his four-volume *The Traditional Tunes of the Child Ballads* (1959-72). Child and Bronson are the Gilbert and Sullivan of balladry: they have provided, between them, the words and the music. In the introduction to his anthology of tunes, Bronson gave this rhetorical exchange:

Question: When is a ballad not a ballad?
Answer: When it has no tune.

This is now the modern orthodoxy. Yet if we are not to regress infinitely to the sterile conclusion that a ballad is a ballad is a ballad we have to accept the versatility of the term. The ballad can accept any number of epithets, and there are tuneless ballads as well as broadside ballads and popular ballads and literary ballads. Perhaps the final distinction will be that crucial one between good ballads and bad ballads.

2
Style of the ballads

I shall omit everything that is not strictly a Popular Ballad.
(Francis James Child, letter of 4 January
1875 to Sven Grundtvig)

Sir Walter Scott, a professional poet who made a fortune out
of narrative verse before applying his talents to the historical
novel, was extremely critical of what he took to be a lack of
artistic integrity on the part of the ballad makers. In his 'Intro-
ductory Remarks on Popular Poetry' appended to the 1830 edition of his *Minstrelsy* he positively simmered with moral
indignation:

> The least acquaintance with the subject will recall a great
> number of commonplace verses, which each ballad-maker
> has unceremoniously appropriated to himself, thereby
> greatly facilitating his own task, and at the same time
> degrading his art by his slovenly use of over-scutched
> phrases.

If the ballad-makers had been, like Scott, professional poets
aiming at the immortality of print, then this criticism would be
apposite. In ballad after ballad the same narrative method is
sustained and the similarity goes right down to details like the
obligatory epithets in 'milk-white steed', 'blood-red wine', 'wan
water'.

Because he thought, with Percy, that the popular ballads
had been composed by professional minstrels, Scott felt justi-
fied in his charge of unashamed plagiarism. Yet the ballad style

is the result not of a literary progression of innovators and their acolytes but of the evolution of a form that could be mentally absorbed by practitioners of an oral idiom made for the memory. To survive, the ballad had to have a repertoire of mnemonic devices. Ballad singers knew not one but a whole host of ballads (Mrs Brown of Falkland knew thirty-three separate ballads). So the similarity of the ballads is the result of a successful tradition, not of literary theft as Scott implied.

Obviously the basic structure had to be sound. The metre of the ballads ensures this. The pattern widely known as the ballad stanza is an abcb quatrain in which four-stress and three-stress lines alternate thus (79A):

> There lived a wife at Usher's Well,
> And a wealthy wife was she;
> She had three stout and stalwart sons,
> And sent them oer the sea.

This pattern is used in 179 of Child's 305 ballads and has become synonymous with balladry. According to Gerould, who has closely examined the Grieg and Sharp collections of tunes, this is not a quatrain but 'quite certainly a couplet with seven stresses to the line' *(The Ballad of Tradition,* p. 125). Though the melodic cadence bears this out, it is immaterial: the ballad stanza is an accepted typographical convention and is here to stay. The next most common metric entity in balladry is the four-stress line which is used in 111 Child ballads. Child's earliest ballad examples use four-stress couplets, for example 'Riddles Wisely Expounded' (1A):

> The youngest daughter that same night,
> She went to bed to this young knight.

Most of the four-stress lines are arranged in abcb quatrains.

Child's criterion was that to be popular a ballad had to be orally composed: in his headnote to 'The Laily Worm and the Machrel of the Sea' (36) he said 'it is pure tradition, and has never been retouched by a pen'. He was, though, obliged to rely on broadside texts for many of his ballads and rationalized this by claiming these were decadent versions of once genuinely popular ballads. As Child made his collection from extant collections, broadsides and, to a lesser extent, manuscripts — rather than from actual singers — it is difficult to estimate the role of the refrain in the ballads, though around half of them carry refrains. These must have been a musical part and parcel of the idiom. 'The Cruel Mother' (20B) has an internal refrain —

> She sat down below a thorn,
>> Fine flowers in the valley
> And there she has her sweet babe born.
>> And the green leaves they grow rarely.

— which adds nothing to the narrative but matches the melody. 'The Elfin Knight' (2A) has both an internal refrain and an external burden which is longer than the narrative stanza, and Child notes that 'this kind of burden seems to have been common enough with old songs and carols'. Poetically the refrains are decorative; musically they are absolutely essential.

The rhymes of the ballads are as predictable as we would expect from an oral phenomenon that depends on memorability. Some are used as a matter of course: in the pining-away ballads of true love one lover fades away and the survivor dies for sorrow on the morrow as in 'Fair Margaret and Sweet William' (74B):

> Lady Margaret died on the over night,
>> Sweet William died on the morrow;
> Lady Margaret died for pure, pure love,
>> Sweet William died for sorrow.

Often the rhymes are technically imperfect — 'Lord Ingram and Chiel Wyet' (66A) has *bower/honour, warm/bairn, man/*-

land — but in musical performance these are resolved by the emphatic cadences which function with the finality of rhyme.

Music had an important formative influence on the ballads, though not all ballads were sung. The most popular ballads acquired a large number of musical variants: Bronson has, for example, sixty-eight different tunes for 'The Maid Freed from the Gallows' (95). Whether the music determined the genesis of the ballad or whether music was subsequently added as a natural refinement and memorable development of the narrative style is one of those almost unanswerable questions that appear endlessly in the pages of ballad criticism. I am inclined to believe that, as the priority of the ballad is the story, the music had a secondary, mnemonic role. Generations of readers, after all, have been content with the words alone, and the same could not be said of the music. As far as the ballads go we might say that in the beginning was the word as an indispensable step to building a story. Cecil Sharp thought the words took precedence in the evolution of the ballad:

> The pattern of the folk tune has, throughout its evolution been dominated by the words with which at first it was probably always associated. . . . The unit of musical form is . . . the proportioned melody; and that most certainly took shape under the controlling influence of the metrical structure of the words to which it was united.
>
> *(English Folk Song,* p. 92)

Bronson, who has succeeded Sharp as the supreme authority on ballad music, feels that, on the contrary, 'It is the music which has dictated and controlled the stanzaic habit of ballads. . . . The music, again, has governed the strategy of the dialogue in ballads.' *(The Traditional Tunes of the Child Ballads,* Vol. I, pp. ix-x.) That two great scholars could differ on such a fundamental issue reveals the problematic nature of ballad studies.

Unlike the chromatic scale employed by the composers of art music, folk music used seven diatonic modes. By playing only the white, or natural, notes of the piano the seven modes can be heard thus: *Dorian* (D-E-F-G-A-B-C-D), *Phrygian* (E-F-G-A-B-C-D-E), *Lydian* (F-G-A-B-C-D-E-F), *Mixolydian* (G-A-B-C-D-E-F-G), *Aeolian* (A-B-C-D-E-F-G-A: the natural minor), *Locrian* (B-C-D-E-F-G-A-B), *Ionian* (C-D-E-F-G-A-B-C: the natural major). To hear the distinctive intervals of the modes even more clearly, they can all be referred to the same tonic, thus: *Dorian* (C-D-Eb-F-G-A-Bb-C), *Phrygian* (C-Db-Eb-F-G-Ab-Bb-C), *Lydian* (C-D-E-F#-G-A-B-C), *Mixolydian* (C-D-E-F-G-A-Bb-C), *Aeolian* (C-D-Eb-F-G-Ab-Bb-C), *Locrian* (C-Db-Eb-F-Gb-Ab-Bb-C), *Ionian* (C-D-E-F-G-A-B-C). Although the modes are potentially heptatonic (seven-noted), the singers of ballads were drawn to pentatonic (five-noted) and hexatonic (six-noted) melodies.

To the musically illiterate the musicological exposition of modality can sound forbidding; the tunes themselves, thankfully, do not. The listener experiences the strophic melody in waves that alter subtly with each step of the narrative as the singer exercises a re-creative prerogative. Ballad music was monodic, as the basic story had to unfold without extraneous and distracting accompaniment. Something of the original quality of the ballads can be heard in the many recordings made by great modern ballad singers such as Ewan MacColl or Jeanie Robertson. The stark melancholy of the great popular ballads imposes itself on the listener as the solo voice gives a quintessentially human presence to the performance. Ballads, in this sense, represent the art of storytelling raised to a musical pitch.

It is an extraordinary art of storytelling. It is intensely dramatic, involving an explosive situation, highly volatile characters and a short time-span. Given the situation in almost any ballad, something is *bound* to happen. When the lord leaves his castle in 'Lamkin' (93) we know he is asking for trouble; when Lady Barnard summons Little Musgrave to her bed (81) a tragic conclusion is certain; when the lady responds to the gypsies at her door in 'The Gypsy Laddie' (200) she is courting trouble. Like classical tragedy the ballads have an inevitability which reflects the folk belief that fate shapes human life so that people are lured into the fatally attractive traps. Like classical tragedy too the fact that the audience are likely to have heard the story before makes little difference; the tale can stand repeated tellings and the ballad style is responsible for this. It is satisfying to the ear and its regular beat reassures the heart.

It has been well established that the popular ballads were created, in the first place, by unlettered folk who evolved an oral idiom appropriate to the stories they wanted to preserve. Whether they also created the stories is irrelevant: nobody thinks any the less of Shakespeare because he lifted his plots from other sources. The impersonality of the ballads precludes a definite point of view; the frequent parade of great wealth in the stories probably gave some folk as much vicarious pleasure as it gave others a cause for envy. Yet there are examples of class consciousness in the ballads where our sympathy is engaged on the side of little people who are seen to suffer. In 'Glasgerion' (67) and 'Lady Diamond' (269) the tragedy results from the fact that a lady has slept with a social inferior, and, in 'Lady Diamond' (269) at least, some emotional purchase is obtained from the injustice of taking human life for that. 'Lamkin' (93) too has class implications, though the hideous aspects of the stonemason's character leave us in no doubt that whatever else the ballads are they are not glorifications of one class at the expense of another.

In the popular ballads we discern an overall style, an idiom that testifies to the enormous creative potential of the folk. Many of the difficulties socially privileged critics have imposed on the ballads derive from their reluctance to credit the so-called lower classes with creative genius. Yet they have always possessed it, and it has produced phenomena like the autodidact Robert Burns, like the astonishingly inventive black jazz musicians of America to whom improvization seems like second nature, like the best of the British pop musicians of the 1960s. The great ballads were made by unsung singers, anonymous amateurs — though we should remember, as A. L. Lloyd puts it, that 'The famous anonymity of folk-song is, in the main, an economic and social accident'. *(Folk Song in England,* p. 24).

It is the popular style that we are concerned with here. The broadside will be examined in another chapter and the minstrel ballad is really the popular ballad writ vulgar. Lacking the intrinsic stylistic dignity of popular balladry, the minstrels relied on professional tricks and ear-catching patter; the opening of 'Robin Hood and Allen a Dale' (138) is fairly typical:

> Come listen to me, you gallants so free,
>> All you that loves mirth for to hear,
> And I will you tell of a bold outlaw,
>> That lived in Nottinghamshire.

In passing it should be said that one modern critic has given a much higher status than is usual to the minstrels. Fowler believes that the Robin Hood ballads were the most popular, most enduring creation of the minstrelsy in the fifteenth and sixteenth centuries and, moreover, that these ballads created a stylistic precedent for the creation of new popular ballads in the seventeenth and eighteenth centuries. They showed the way for the popular music. Fowler is convinced that 'without the impetus of the Robin Hood repertoire the popular ballad would never have come into being'. *(A Literary History of the Popular Ballad,* p. 65).

'Judas' (23), the earliest English ballad preserved in writing, has often had doubts cast on its ballad pedigree, but it displays the features of the real thing. There is no lengthy exposition; instead we are plunged *in medias res.* It is swift and to the point, it admits no irrelevant details, and it relies on dialogue:

> Hit wes upon a Scere-thorsday that ure loverd aros;
> Ful milde were the wordes he spec to Judas.

'Judas, thou most to Jerusalem, oure mete for to bugge;
Thritt platen of selver thou bere up othi rugge.'

Ballad stories tend to be autonomous — that is, they contain in themselves the information they explore. They do not seek historical or, in this case, biblical accuracy. Here Judas, having been given the thirty pieces of silver to buy food in Jerusalem, is lulled to sleep by his sister. He wakes to find the silver gone and when Pilate approaches him he considers selling his Lord in order to recover the lost silver. This makes Judas more a foolish man of the people than a theological bogeyman. The eighteen couplets that comprise 'Judas' (23) are vivid, impersonal, dramatic, rhythmically simple: these qualities make up a genuine ballad.

A much later ballad, 'Earl Brand' (7C), which Child extracted from Motherwell's manuscripts, displays a number of features which have come to be regarded as hallmarks of the ballad style. The opening quatrain is dramatic, is in direct speech, uses the magical number seven, and contains the essential facts of the explosive situation:

'Rise up, rise up, my seven brave sons,
    And dress in your armour so bright;
Earl Douglas will hae Lady Margaret away
    Before that it be light.'

The action takes off with the speed of the finest milk-white ballad steed and by the third stanza Earl Douglas is preparing to defend his conquest by fighting Lady Margaret's father and seven brothers. This willingness to take on impossible odds — one man against eight — exemplifies the hyperbolic texture of the ballads. Earl Douglas, after his amazing triumph in battle, lifts his lady on the omnipresent 'milk-white steed' and himself on the complementary 'dapple grey' and they ride on to the usual wan water:

They rode, they rode, and they better rode,
    Till they came to yon water wan;

> They lighted down to gie their horse a drink
>> Out of the running stream.

Now the majority of ballads have a romantic and/or tragic dimension and the ballad folk would not expect Earl Douglas to carry his lady off and live happy ever after. She, in fact, perceives proleptically that 'ye are slain'. Accordingly he rides home to that familiar ballad figure, the omnipotent matriarch, to await his death. His request to his mother illustrates the imitative response that is one of the commonplaces of the ballad style:

> 'O rise, dear mother, and make my bed,
>> And make it braid and wide,
> And lay me down to take my rest,
>> And at my back my bride.'

> She has risen and made his bed,
>> She made it braid and wide;
> She laid him down to take his rest,
>> And at his back his bride.

It is a *sine qua non* of romantic tragic balladry that if one lover dies the other must follow suit, so he dies of his wound and she of sorrow (conveniently rhyming with morrow).

That, however, is not the end of the story, for convention requires a rose-and-briar ending. This must have given a satisfactory flourish of a finale to the romantic ballads: the entwining of the plants is a much-loved symbolic monument to true love.

> The one was buried in Mary's kirk,
>> The other in Mary's quire;
> The one sprung up a bonnie bush,
>> And the other a bonny brier.

> These twa grew, and these twa threw,
>> Till they came to the top,

> And when they could na farther gae,
>> They coost the lovers' knot.

The features we have observed in this ballad can be seen in scores of others. A man with these effects at his command was perfectly equipped to learn and carry a new ballad and to reproduce it according to time-tested formulas.

F. B. Gummere, whose adherence to choral origins and communal composition have made him a rather dated figure in the discussion of the ballad, is associated with two critical terms that accurately describe key stylistic features of balladry: *leaping and lingering* and *incremental repetition*. The leaping and lingering of balladry refers to its tendency to initiate a sudden act and then to linger hypnotically after the event. In 'Clerk Saunders' (69B) the amorous thought that leaps to the hero's mind is precisely stated:

> 'A bed, a bed,' Clerk Saunders said,
>> 'And ay a bed for you and me';
> 'Never a ane', said the gay lady,
>> 'Till ance we twa married be.'

She then mentions the passionate jealousy of her seven brothers and he, in response, suggests that she blindfold herself and carry him to bed so she can claim she never saw him, neither did his feet touch her bedroom floor. They linger over this ploy for five stanzas while suspense is being built up.

Incremental repetition is probably the most readily identifiable of ballad characteristics. By this device a stanza repeats the previous stanza with some significant addition that advances the narrative. This can be used with devastating ironical effect, as in 'The Bonny Earl of Murray' (181A), or more dramatically as in the incest ballad 'Lizie Wan' (51A). The listener is led to think by the end of the second quatrain that the cause of grief is an unwanted pregnancy; by altering the reiteration the ballad soon displays a greater taboo than illegitimacy:

Lizie Wan sits at her father's bower-door,
   Weeping and making a mane,
And by there came her father dear:
   'What ails thee, Lizie Wan?'

'I ail, and I ail, dear father,' she said,
   'And I'll tell you a reason for why;
There is a child between my twa sides,
   Between my dear billy and I.'

Now Lizie Wan sits at her father's bower-door,
   Sighing and making a mane,
And by there came her brother dear:
   'What ails thee, Lizie Wan?'

'I ail, I ail, dear brither,' she said,
   'And I'll tell you a reason for why;
There is a child between my two sides,
   Between you, dear billy, and I.'

Incremental repetition is a superlative mnemonic technique, and the structural beauty of the form must have prompted some fine ballad compositions. One, 'The Maid Freed from the Gallows' (95A), is entirely determined by incremental repetition. It comprises five sets of three linked quatrains. We are suddenly plunged into a catastrophic situation whereby a maid is pleading for her life. No crime is specified, if crime it be, since ransom will easily free her. This is the basic three-quatrain pattern:

'O good Lord Judge, and sweet Lord Judge,
   Peace for a little while:
Methinks I see my own father,
   Come riding by the stile.

'Oh father, oh father, a little of your gold,
   And likewise of your fee!
To keep my body from yonder grave,
   And my neck from the gallows-tree.'

> 'None of my gold now you shall have,
> Nor likewise of my fee;
> For I am come to see you hangd,
> And hanged you shall be.'

The pattern is repeated as the girl appeals to her mother, her brother, her sister. It is only her final appeal, to her lover, that succeeds, so his reply is significantly different:

> 'Some of my gold now you shall have,
> And likewise of my fee,
> For I am come to see you saved,
> And saved you shall be.'

To memorize a ballad like this one the singer's mind could lock on to the three-quatrain pattern.

Another feature which sustains ballad narrative in a memorable way is the nuncupative testament. A dying or departing protagonist is asked to dispose of his or her possessions and does so in a particularly telling fashion. This is not a simple shareout of goods to the family but has ironic overtones, for the villain of the piece is left a curse instead of a commodity. In 'The Cruel Brother' (11A) the beautiful fair-haired heroine is stabbed by her brother John, who is furious at not being asked to consent to her choice of husband. The dying heroine says

> 'O lead me gently up yon hill,
> And I'll there sit down, and make my will.'

She leaves her 'silver-shod steed' to her father, her 'velvet pall and . . . silken gear' to her mother, her 'silken scarf and . . . gowden fan' to her sister Anne, her 'bloody cloaths' to her sister Grace. As for the murderer:

> 'What will you leave to your brother John?'
> 'The gallows-tree to hang him on.'

The testament also plays its part in 'Lord Randal' (12A), a ballad uniquely built for oral survival. It has perhaps the most memorable pattern of any ballad, as can be seen if we quote the first quatrain and italicize the only parts that alter in the subsequent nine quatrains:

> '*O where ha you been,* Lord Randal, my son?
> *And where ha you been,* my handsome young man?'
> '*I ha been at the greenwood;* mother, mak my bed soon.'
> For I'm wearied wi hunting, and fain wad lie down.'

The result of the iteration is to give the narrative an almost intolerable urgency; the insistent demand for the deathbed suggests the imminence of the young lord's death. After admitting he has been poisoned by his true love he makes his nuncupative testament leaving livestock to his mother, jewellery to his sister, property to his brother and 'hell and fire' to his homicidal sweetheart.

'Edward' (13B) contains the most celebrated and controversial use of the nuncupative testament in balladry. 'The Cruel Brother' (11A) and 'Lord Randal' (12A) put the testament in the mouths of murder victims so that the final curse is unavoidable. Whereas these ballads are relatively ingenuous, 'Edward' (13B) is incredibly ingenious and does not yield its secret until the very last line. As the ballad opens Edward is being interrogated by his mother who is determined to discover the source of the blood on his sword. After some evasion Edward admits he has murdered his father and the mother then prompts him for the testament. Instead of the gradual build-up to a conventional curse there is something altogether stronger, for Edward leaves his land to decay and his family to starve; as for his mother:

> 'The curse of hell frae me sall ye beir,
> Mither, mither,
> The curse of hell frae me sall ye beir,
> Sic counseils ye gave to me O.'

That desolate shock-ending, which implicates the mother as instigator of the crime, is untypical of the ballads generally, where amazing events follow given facts. In 'Edward' (13B) the crucial fact is concealed until the last moment. So unusual is 'Edward' (13B) that Bronson *(The Ballad as Song,* pp. 1-17) has doubted its authenticity. The ballad was sent to Percy by Sir David Dalrymple, Lord Hailes, and Bronson suspects that he was responsible for the literary cunning of 'Edward' (13B). It seems to Bronson altogether too good — in a contrived literary sense — to be a true ballad. Against this we have to set Child's opinion that 'Edward' (13B) 'is not only unimpeachable, but has ever been regarded as one of the noblest and most sterling specimens of the popular ballad'. I think we have to trust Child's ear rather than Bronson's nose for a controversy.

It is likely that Bronson, in his mission to establish the supremacy of tunes, has underestimated the verbal magic of balladry. Yet the words alone do so much. There is the use of irony in 'The Bonny Earl of Murray' (181A), the slow construction of tension in 'The Lass of Roch Royal' (76B), the poetic use of the ominous dream in 'The Battle of Otterburn' (161C), the brooding imagery of revenant ballads like 'The Unquiet Grave' (78), the exquisite melancholy of 'The Great Silkie of Sule Skerry' (113), the romantic poignancy of 'The Gypsy Laddie' (200). A tradition that was capable of such peaks of verbal and structural perfection was capable of 'Edward' (13B). I do not doubt that the ballad was composed by an individual (another anonymous amateur) but I doubt that the individual was Lord Hailes; if he had been responsible for it, then commonsense decrees that he would have eventually stood forward to claim credit for his masterwork.

Felicitous details are the exception, not the rule, in balladry. It could not be otherwise, for the creators of ballads were not poetic innovators but members of a community working within the confines of an all-purpose oral idiom. The ballad style had to serve a whole host of individuals, had to ring as true in London as it did in Aberdeen, had to have an unbreakable formal structure. So most ballad characteristics are big overall effects, features that could be swallowed whole and regurgitated in a recognizable manner. The ballad style is hyperbolic; actions and events are exaggerated so they will appear more vivid. It is this that gives rise to some of the more extreme images. In 'Lord Thomas and Fair Annet' (73D) the hero's wife, the brown girl, murders his lover; the hero's reaction is instant:

> Lord Thomas he had a sword by his side,
> As he walked about the hall;
> He cut off his bride's head from her shoulders,
> And he threw it against the wall.

After Lord Burnard has decapitated the youth in 'Child Maurice' (83D) — in the belief that he is his lady's lover when, in fact, he is his lady's son — he presents the severed head for use as a football:

> He's put it in a braid basin,
> And brocht it in the ha,
> And laid it in his lady's lap;
> 'Said, Lady, tak a ba!'

> 'Play ye, play ye, my lady,' he said,
> 'Play ye frae ha to bower;
> Play ye wi Gill Morice head,
> He was your paramour.'

It is as if the scenes were visualised, in the mind's eye, in chiaroscuro. Terrible dark shadows alternate with brilliant highlights. Because of the absence of characterization the force of the anecdote has to be concentrated into action. At times this becomes almost bathetic. The eponymous heroine of 'Lady Isabel and the Elf-Knight' (4B) is credited with incredible strength in her battle against her adversary:

> She's taen him in her arms twa,
> An thrown him headlong in.

The most famous hyperbolic image occurs in Chevy Chase —
'The Hunting of the Cheviot' (162B) — when we are told:

> For Witherington needs must I wayle
>   as one in dolefull dumpes,
> For when his leggs were smitten of,
>   he fought upon his stumpes.

Samuel Butler incorporated this image in *Hudibras,* as it fitted
in perfectly with his mock-heroic manner:

> Enraged thus some in the rear
> Attack'd him, and some ev'ry where;
> Till down he fell, yet falling fought,
> And being down still laid about;
> As *Widdrington* in doleful Dumps
> Is said to fight upon his stumps.
>
> (I. iii. 91-6)

In all fairness to Sidney, whose name has been associated with
'Chevy Chase' as its first influential eulogist, it should be said
that he was probably acquainted with Child's A text which has
the more credible version:

> For Wetharryngton my harte was wo,
>   that ever he slayne shulde be;
> For when both his leggis wear hewyne in to,
>   yet he knyled and fought on hys kny.

The B text is a broadside vulgarization of the A text.

A Witherington-inspired feat occurs in 'Johnie Cock'
(114A) which Child called a 'precious specimen of the
unspoiled traditional ballad'. Seven foresters attack the outlaw
Johnie:

> O the first stroke that they gae him,
>   They struck him off by the knee;

Still, Johnie kills six of his seven attackers. More outrageous
heroism is recounted in 'Johnnie Armstrong' (169B):

> Said John, Fight on, my merry men all,
>   I am a little hurt, but I am not slain;
> I will lay me down for to bleed a while,
>   Then I'le rise and fight with you again.

This hyperbolic style partly comes from a desire to astonish; we can imagine how poor folk would delightedly turn from their hard work to hear of the larger-than-life exploits of ballad people. Also the vicarious pleasure they would derive from great displays of wealth. 'Young Beichan' (53A) would have appealed not only as an exotic adventure story but because of the sumptuous parade of wealth, for when Shusy Pye comes after her recalcitrant lover the porter describes her appearance:

> 'For on every finger she has a ring,
>   An on the mid-finger she has three,
> An there's as meikle goud aboon her brow
>   As woud buy an earldome o lan to me.'

Such images would have glistened in the eyes of many a person who listened to a ballad in a penurious environment.

Balladry is an art of contrast and counterpoint, the black balancing with the milk-white. A familiar touch is the combination of antithetical emotions in one quatrain, as in 'Mary Hamilton' (173I):

> When she cam to the Netherbow Port,
>   She laughed loud laughters three;
> But when she cam to the gallows-foot,
>   The tears blinded her ee.

As if to emphasize the sacrifice she has made, the lady of 'The Gypsy Laddie' (200B) draws this contrast:

> 'Last night I lay in a weel-made bed,
>   And my noble lord beside me,
> And now I must ly in an old tenant's-barn,
>   And the black crew glowring owre me.'

The use of counterpoint is a useful textural device: the colour of gold is good and the golden-haired lady most desirable of all; the colour of earth is suspect and a dark person is devious (we should remember that Shusy Pye redeemed her colour by an ostentatious display of golden jewellery). Hence the dubious role of love-breaker attributed to the nut-brown girl in the ballads. In 'Lord Thomas and Fair Annet' (73) his lordship marries the nut-brown girl for her money instead of taking Annet for her bright beauty. In 'Fair Margaret and Sweet William' (74) William's marriage to the nut-brown girl drives Margaret to suicide.

This discussion has isolated only the major stylistic similarities between the ballads, but there are many more minor features — like the household familiar Billy Blin who appears in 'Young Beichan' (53C) and 'Willie's Lady' (6A) or the talking bird. In 'Lady Isabel and the Elf-Knight' (4C) a parrot witnesses the murder and May Colven (an incarnation of Lady Isabel) offers it a golden cup and fine cage for its silence; in 'Young Hunting' (68C) the homicidal lady offers the parrot, or bonny bird, a golden cage if it will keep quiet. The bird in 'The Gay Goshawk' (96A) takes a message south to its master's sweetheart imploring her to join him in Scotland. (Her father being against the match, the girl secures from him a promise that she be buried in Scotland, then takes a sleeping draught which enables her to be resuscitated in the arms of her lover.) 'The Carnal and the Crane' (55) reproduces a theological discussion between two talking birds, while the ornithological discourse in 'The Three Ravens' (26) and 'The Twa Corbies' (given by Child in his headnote to No. 26) concerns the corpse they want to make a meal of.

It is perhaps appropriate to close this account of ballad stylistics with yet another convention — the Last Goodnight. This allows a character to bid a fond farewell to the world. It became a hackneyed standby of the broadside ballads; for, before public executions were banned in Britain in 1866, the ballad-sellers would sell their wares at the scene of the execution. In the popular ballads the Last Goodnight has the more poetic purpose of allowing a brave man to give a final display of courage. Such is the case in 'Hobie Noble' (189) and in 'Johnie Armstrong' (169B) where the Border hero bids a defiant goodbye to life:

> 'And God be withee, Kirsty, my son,
>   Whair thou sits on thy nurses knee!
> But and thou live this hundred yeir,
>   Thy fathers better thoult never be.'

3
Content of the ballads

> Strictness is offensive as well as useless. Perhaps it is impossible.
> Ballads are not like plants or insects, to be classified to a hair's
> breadth.
>
> (Francis James Child, Child MSS, Harvard
> Library, Vol. XXIV, pp. 468-9)

The picture painted by Percy, and retouched by Scott, of illustrious minstrels entertaining great lords and ladies in their halls was shown by Ritson and subsequent scholars to have been a false impression. We now distinguish between minstrel and popular ballads and find the minstrels artistically inferior to traditional balladry. But who sang the popular ballads? Do the magical elements in them indicate a credulous peasantry possessed by a collective belief in superstitious irrationality? These are not rhetorical questions, for many scholars are so ready to attribute dark ignorance to the ballad folk that we are in danger of reading between the lines of the ballads to reconstruct a complete folk cosmology.

In many ways the ballads became old wives' tales, and I do not mean this in any pejorative sense. They were stories passed from mother to daughter, perpetuated by women. In John Barbour's fourteenth-century vernacular epic *The Brus* there is a reference to a ballad:

> Young women quhen thai will play,
> Syng it amang thaim ilka day.
>
> (xvi. 521-2)

In Shakespeare's *Twelfth Night* (II. iv) the Duke requests an old song:

> The spinsters and the knitters in the sun,
> And the free maids, that weave their thread with bones,
> Do use to chant it . . .

John Aubrey (1626-97) said that 'In the old ignorant times before women were Readers, ye [ballads] was handed downe from mother to daughter, &c . . . So my nurse has the history from the conquest downe to Carl. I in ballad' (quoted in Palmer, *A Touch on the Times,* p. 18). We know that Mrs Brown of Falkland learned her songs from her mother, her nurse and her aunt, while Charles Kirkpatrick Sharpe's *A Ballad Book* (1823) begins with a note to the 'Courteous Reader' explaining that 'These have been mostly gathered from the mouths of nurses, wet and dry, singing to their babes and sucklings, dairymaids pursuing their vocation in the cow-house, and tenants' daughters, while giving the Lady . . . a spinning day.' William Chappell, in his *Popular Music of the Olden Time* (1855-9), said that 'Tinkers sang catches; milkmaids sang ballads'; invariably when a ballad has been collected from tradition the source is female. Sir Walter Scott learned much about balladry from Mrs Hogg, the mother of the Ettrick Shepherd.

The matriarch is a powerful and awesome figure in balladry and this is relevant to the fact that women were so often the custodians of the oral tradition. In 'Gil Brenton' (5A), one of Mrs Brown's ballads, the kingly hero has brought home a wife who, learning that his custom is to murder any unchaste spouse (and he's had seven of them), hires a virgin to take her place in the bridal bed. Gil Brenton asks his bedclothes if he has married a maid and the talking sheets truthfully reply:

> 'It's nae a maid that you ha wedded,
> But it's a maid that you ha bedded.'

At this Gil Brenton rushes to his mother to relate the dreadful news and the formidable 'auld queen' knocks down the new bride's door and demands to know who is the father of her child. The lady explains that she, one of seven sisters, worked for seven years on a sark for the king's son; one day in the greenwood to pull the nut and the sloe (a fairy summons) she was seduced by a lover who left her some love-tokens. Recognizing these as the property of her son the auld queen reunites the pair. When Fair Ellen of 'Child Waters' (63A) — a ballad Child considered to have 'no superior in English' — tells Child Waters she is carrying his baby she is treated to verbal and physical abuse. He condescends to take her home disguised as his foot-page and she has to walk, then swim a river, while he rides. He even sends her into town to find a beautiful woman for his bed before she retires to the stables. There, in labour, she moans and Child Waters's mother comes to her rescue by sending her son to his woman. The ballad ends happily in marriage.

If ballad singing was so often undertaken by women it is possible that it was thought unseemly for a man to spend his time on ballads — which supports Ritson's assessment of the minstrels and the generally contemptuous attitude to male balladmongers. There were exceptions: at one time the only living open to a blind man was music and this disability would promote the cultivation of a phenomenal memory. One thinks of the blind fiddler who so moved Sir Philip Sidney by his performance of 'The Hunting of the Cheviot' (162A), even of the 'silly blind harper' who stole King Henry's horse in 'The Lochmaber Harper' (192A).

Peter Buchan, the mendacious publisher whose ballads Child reluctantly canonized, employed a blind beggar to obtain his material. Born blind in 1770 in Aberdeenshire, James Rankin turned to begging on the death of his father in 1825. He was soon in the service of Buchan who wrote, in a letter of 16 February to Motherwell:

I sent for and brought an old blind man from a great distance [actually only fifteen miles from Strichen], kept him in Peterhead for upwards of four weeks [actually one week], and paid all expenses, besides of his own charges, which were not inconsiderable . . . He was, however, worthy of his reward, great as it was, if I could have afforded it, for he was without doubt, a second Homer. He was possessed of the best memory I ever knew . . .

According to Bell Robertson — the Aberdeenshire woman who contributed almost 400 songs to Gavin Grieg — Rankin was far from being a second Homer. She said:

His memory was very remarkable, he had a large stock of ballads and songs, but was distinctly of low intelligence. . . . Being blind, he learned everything from someone's saying or singing, and probably did not know whether it was sung from a printed copy or from memory and tradition. The idea of Jamie making up anything himself was considered absurd.

(In William Walker, *Peter Buchan and Other Papers* (1915), p. 59)

The amazing memory of blind singers was also noted by Cecil Sharp:

. . . a blind man, one Mr Henry Larcombe, also from Haselbury-Plucknett, sang me a Robin Hood ballad. The words consisted of eleven verses. These proved to be almost word for word the same as the corresponding stanzas of a much longer black-letter broadside preserved in the Bodleian Library.

(*English Folk Song,* p. 22)

Blind men, then, appear to have learned ballads parrot-fashion from someone who knew a broadside or remembered the piece. They were not creators. Women, though, were the most prominent carriers of oral balladry. They were also capable of creating individual variants, as the case of Mrs Brown of Falkland has shown.

These ballad-singers would wish to provide exciting stories, extraordinary tales whose easily assimilated narrative substance would provide a welcome means of escape from the predictable rhythms of ordinary life. Today, when scientific knowledge is accessible to all, we have become conditioned to an empirical assessment of life and can provide at least a partial cause for every effect. We rely on information; the non-literate folk relied on imagination. Folklore, in this context, is really an imaginative interpretation of an apparently random universe. In the absence of an established scientific order the folk had to rely on entertainment which they nevertheless took very seriously indeed. This is not to say that the ballads were treated as metaphysical gospel. The ballad folk were sufficiently rooted in the reality of their harsh rural world to accept that life rambled on without the intervention of ghosts and grotesques. They were often naive but not hopelessly credulous, totally at the mercy of superstition. They could not have coped with life if they were. For them the ballads were not an exact record of their outlook; they were, first and last, entertaining stories.

In his list of the most popular ballads Bronson compiles the following chart:

1 'Bonny Barbara Allan' (84)
2 'Lord Thomas and Fair Annet' (73)
3 'Lord Randal' (12)
4 'Lady Isabel and the Elf-Knight' (4)
5 'The Gypsy Laddie' (200)
6 'Young Beichan' (53)
7 'James Harris' ('The Daemon Lover') (243)
(*The Ballad as Song*, pp. 162-70)

Now this contains stories of, respectively, tragic love; the eternal triangle; murder; magic; romantic passion; requited love;

the supernatural. It has, in fact, the same thematic mix we would find in a modern chart of bestsellers. The ballad folk were, in their appetite for fiction, much like us. Consider what would happen if some anti-cultural weapon destroyed all public libraries but spared the reading material in private homes. On the evidence of domestic bookshelves alone we could be condemned as a superstitious, credulous society hopelessly addicted to ghost stories, murder mysteries, romantic fiction, supernatural thrillers, and the like. Yet most of us do not actually believe in ghosts, monsters and mutants; we simply like hearing about them. It was the same with the folk who listened to the ballads. They enjoyed good stories. Unless, like the communalists, we want to push the origins of the ballad back to some nameless antiquity, we should remember that the ballads flourished in the Renaissance period and were enjoyed during the Age of Reason. We are dealing with stories so gripping that they have retained their popularity to the present day. I am not saying there are not relevant remnants of folklore, magic and superstition in the ballads; but rather that their significance has been grossly overestimated.

'Traditionally,' A. L. Lloyd says, 'art music is a diversion for the educated classes, while folk music is one of the most intimate, reassuring and embellishing possessions of the poor' (*Folk Song in England*, p. 17). The stories that were possessed by the folk had to be absorbing, had to engage and stimulate the emotions. They were something naturally acquired by the folk, not imposed on them like religion. For this reason there is a paucity of religious ballads. Those with Christian themes display, with the exception of 'Dives and Lazarus' (56), a non-biblical novelty. 'Judas' (23) has little to do with the biblical character and 'The Cherry-Tree Carol' (54A) would have appeared blasphemous to the determinedly orthodox. It is derived from the Pseudo-Matthew's Gospel (ch. xx) and has a very realistic Joseph. For when Mary asks her elderly husband to pluck her a cherry, Joseph's response is that of a man who suspects his wife has betrayed him:

> O then bespoke Joseph,
>   with words most unkind:
> 'Let him pluck thee a cherry
>   that brought thee with child.'

The tension is resolved when Christ speaks from the womb and the cherry-tree bends to his will.

Both 'Saint Stephen and Herod' (22) and 'The Carnal and the Crane' (55) have a roasted cock miraculously announcing Christ's nativity, a magical touch that would have delighted the folk. An even more unusual portrayal of the Christian saga illuminated 'The Bitter Withy', a ballad unknown to Child. Here Christ is made painfully aware of his humble social status when three boys refuse to allow him to join them at football:

> 'Oh, we are lords' and ladies' sons,
>   Born in bower or in hall,
> And You are some poor maid's child
>   Born'd in an ox's stall.'

Christ's un-Christian reaction to this taunt is to build a bridge of sunbeams which dissolve under the feet of the three supercilious children so that they drown. A far from meek-and-mild Mary decides to punish Christ for this by chastising him with the withy (willow):

> Mary mild, Mary mild, called home her Child,
>   And laid our Saviour across her knee,
> And with a whole handful of bitter withy
>   She gave him slashes three.

The popular ballads are remarkably free from religious dogma, and it was only when the idiom was in decline that ecclesiastical allusions were clamped on them. Bell Robertson's version of 'Sir Patrick Spens' (58) has this awkward stanza:

> An' four-and-twenty gay ladies
>   Wi their bibles in their han',
> They steed waitin Patrick Spens,
>   Come sailin to dry lan'.
>   (In Buchan, *A Scottish Ballad Book,* p. 153)

These bibles have been put there by wishful thinking, not by tradition, for the popular ballads display a frank sensuality and
an amoral earthiness. Unsurprisingly the majority of them deal
with sex and violence.

The first ballad in Child's collection is 'Riddles Wisely
Expounded', which exemplifies the verbal duel, the contest of
wits, so popular with ballad singers. Often the riddle ballads
show that ordinary folk are not so easily outwitted, not so stu-
pid as they might at first appear. In the oldest version of 'Riddles Wisely Explounded' (1A) a maid escapes the clutches of
the devil by answering his riddles; in a later version (1C) the
maid is unaware of the diabolic nature of her interlocutor,
though fortunately she knows that the answer to

> 'O what is heigher nor the tree?
> And what is deeper nor the sea?'

is

> 'O heaven is higher nor the tree,
> And hell is deeper nor the sea.'

A similar notion is utilized in 'The Fause Knight upon the
Road' (3) in which a child outdoes the devil in a contest of wits.

'Captain Wedderburn's Courtship' (46A) extends the riddling idea into the sexual realm. The captain is irresistibly
attracted to the beautiful lady and insists she come to his bed
and lie against the wall. (Incidentally, Willa Muir (*Living with
Ballads,* p. 37) records that this was the first ballad she ever
heard, in 1906, and felt 'a faint ruffle of embarrassment' when
the sexual theme was introduced.) The lady tries to outwit the
captain with riddles but he is equal to the task: when she asks

for a stoneless cherry he offers a cherry-blossom; when she wants a boneless chicken he offers an egg. Moreover he knows that heaven is higher than a tree and that hell is deeper than the sea. In the end, though, the lady has a matrimonial triumph:

> For now she's Captain Wetherburn's wife,
> a man she never saw,
> And she man lye in his bed, but she'll not
> lye neist the wa.

The contest of wits becomes a battle of the sexes in some ballad pastourelles where country girls outsmart their so-called social betters. In 'The Baffled Knight' (112) a country girl easily escapes the intended embrace of an ardent knight; in 'The Knight and the Shepherd's Daughter' (110) a tenacious shepherdess pursues her knightly seducer to court and demands satisfaction from the king who willingly agrees to a matrimonial solution. The sting is somewhat removed from the tail of this piece when it transpires that the shepherdess is in fact a princess. 'The Broomfield Hill' (43) enlists a witch and a magical spell on the side of the maiden. The amorous knight is strewn with soporific broom blossom and rendered unable to take advantage of the girl when she keeps her tryst with him.

Most ballads do have a sexual dimension; the great exceptions are the English Robin Hood sequence and the Scottish Border sequence. Sometimes the sexuality is present in a tender, romantic, even sentimental way; more often it is explicitly confronted in tales of adultery and uncontrollable passion. In the subdued romantic tragedies lovers tend to pine away and a heart broken by love is the usual way to die. The eponymous hero of 'Lord Love' (75A) leaves his Lady Ouncebell in London while he departs for Scotland. After six months' absence he returns to find the lady has pined away. With impeccable ballad logic he decides to join her in death:

> He caused her corps to be set down,
> And her winding sheet undone,

> And he made a vow before them all
> He'd never kiss woman again.

After a *sorrow/morrow* rhyming quatrain the recognition of 'pure true love' is established by a rose-and-briar ending. The sexual roles are reversed in 'Lady Alice' (85A), for here it is the man who pines away and the lady who dies out of respect for a 'love so true'; again the rose-and-briar convention allows them to unite posthumously.

Supreme among the romantic tragedies is 'Bonny Barbara Allan' (84). Samuel Pepys, in his diary entry for 2 January 1666, said that 'In perfect pleasure I was to hear her [Mrs Knipp, an actress] sing, and especially her little Scotch song of Barbary Allen.' The eternal appeal of this ballad resides in the masterly concision of its narrative. We are told only that the lovers met and parted; that she, after heartlessly hastening his death ('Young man, I think you're dying'), repented and died on the morrow. It is as if the essence of hundreds of romantic love stories had been distilled into this one ballad. The tantalizing lack of details adds an element of mystery to the tragic tale.

The passive, gentle, resigned quality of the pining-away motif contrasts strongly with the erotic honesty of the majority of the sexually motivated ballads. There is no euphemistic avoidance of sex but an absolute delight in its basic presence. A Scottish lady becomes pregnant by an English lord in 'Lady Maisry' (65B), and the opening quatrain could hardly be blunter in its approach to the problem:

> In came her sister,
>   Stepping on the floor;
> Says, It's telling me, my sister Janet,
>   That you're become a whore.

This accusation is repeated by Janet's brother, mother and father. Such ballads are uninhibited, totally free of the literary tradition of courtly love where the woman is an untouchable goddess and the man a willing supplicant before her virginal majesty. In the ballads the lovers are lusty and sexually active. For all that, their amorous actions usually provoke dreadful consequences. 'Lady Diamond' (269A) concerns the love between the heroine and her social inferior, 'a very bonnie kitchen-boy' William:

> He never lay out o Lady Daisy's bower,
>   Till he brought her body to shame.

For this crime he is put to death and, naturally, Lady Diamond (or Daisy or Dysmal or Dysie according to the variant) vows to join him in death.

We must never forget that the folk who most prized the ballads lived in impoverished circumstances, so it should come as no surprise that they enjoyed stories in which the rich come to grief. The Germans have a word for this: *Schadenfreude,* a delight in the discomfort of others. In their everyday lives the ballad folk lurked in the shadows cast by the glorious ostentation of their social betters. Thus in their narrative fantasies it was only to be expected that the fine lords and ladies should experience sensational misfortunes. Through the intervention of popular art the desperately unfair nature of things was balanced out. The poor were pressurized into grinding comformity; apparently the rich made all the rules. If the lords and ladies could take away a large proportion of the wealth produced by the poor then they were not going to escape with impunity in the stories that were possessed by the poor. The lords and ladies were going to be cut down to size, made to suffer for their impulsive actions. They might have all the comforts affluence had to offer; in the seething cauldron of popular art the rich were going to feel the pressure.

Frequently the ballad love-triangle is used to criticize the pursuit of wealth at the expense of love. 'Lord Thomas and Fair Annet' (73A) is an example. Though he loves the beautiful but poor Annet, Lord Thomas marries the rich nut-brown girl. After the wedding poor Annet approaches the couple, only to be unceremoniously stabbed by the nut-brown girl. Lord Thomas then murders his nut-brown wife and stabs himself to death, the whole gory sequence closing on a rose-and-briar finale. Such crimes of passion have enjoyed an oral immortality. 'Young Hunting' (68A) is one of the best of its kind, a tale of murder motivated by jealousy. Young Hunting rather tactlessly tells his sweetheart that he has found a new, more attractive lady; the slighted woman reacts violently:

> And she has minded her on a little penknife,
> That hangs low down by her gare,
> And she has gin him Young Hunting
> A deep wound and a sare.

Afterwards she disposes of the body in the water. This ballad has enjoyed immense popularity in America where Young Hunting has become the luckless Love Henry.

America has also taken 'Little Musgrave and Lady Barnard' (81A) to its heart; in this instance Little Musgrave has been transformed into Matty Groves. The ballad is a great one, a tale of adultery. While Lord Barnard (or Barnett or Barnaby or Barlibas or Bengwill) is absent, his wife approaches Little Musgrave — in church of all places — and asks him home to her bed. Little Musgrave leaps at the offer. A tiny page (the page as bearer of tidings is *de rigueur*) tells all to Lord Barnard who comes back, kills Little Musgrave in a fair fight, then deals with his wife:

> He cut her paps from off her brest;
> Great pitty it was to see
> That some drops of this ladie's heart's blood
> Ran trickling downe her knee.

Not all the love stories end quite as drastically as that. There is the beautifully elegiac 'Geordie' (209) whose sweetheart remains faithful to him even as he is about to be executed; or the lovely 'The Gypsy Laddie' (200B) where the enchanted lady gives up everything for her new man:

'I could sail the seas with my Jockie Faa,
   I could sail the seas with my dearie;
I could sail the seas with my Jockie Faa,
   And with pleasure could drown with my dearie.'

Nor do all the love ballads end tragically. 'Young Beichan' (53A) begins with a wandering Londoner being freed from a fate worse than death by a savage Moor's beautiful daughter, Shusy Pye. With understandable gratitude Beichan promises to return for Shusy in seven years. He does not do so, but takes a wife in London. The indefatigable Shusy tracks him down to his native city and reminds him of his promise. Overcome with emotion, Beichan forsakes his new wife — or rather hands her back to her mother with a double dowry — and marries Shusy, thus changing her name to Lady Jane.

Bronson's list of the seven most popular ballads contains five romantic/passionate ballads: 'Bonny Barbara Allan' (84), 'Lord Thomas and Fair Annet' (73), 'Lord Randal' (12), 'The Gypsy Laddie' (200) and 'Young Beichan' (53). The other two ballads in the list — 'Lady Isabel and the Elf-Knight' (4) and 'James Harris' ('The Daemon Lover') (243) — have their amorous aspects but are usually classified as, respectively, magical and supernatural. 'Lady Isabel and the Elf-Knight' (4) is a truly international ballad: Child felt it had 'perhaps obtained the wildest circulation' of all ballads. There are more than 100 English and American variants, more than 250 German versions, some 80 Polish versions, some 60 French versions and some 50 Hungarian versions. The basic tale is simplicity itself: the lady hears the sound of the elf-knight and longs for his company; he comes and takes her to the greenwood where he informs her she is to die, like the previous seven princesses he has killed; the resourceful Lady Isabel lulls him to sleep and kills him.

'James Harris' ('The Daemon Lover') (243A) is a revenant ballad — that is, it is concerned with a person who returns from the grave not as a disembodied ghost but as a substantial figure: as this ballad puts it, the dead one 'was in human shape, / Much like unto a man'. The ballad relates how a maid marries a carpenter after her lover, James Harris, has died abroad. As a revenant Harris returns for his sweetheart and she, enchanted by him, 'Was never seen no more'. Revenants return for many reasons: for love, for revenge, for peace of mind. 'The Cruel Mother' (20B) has a chilling quality that transcends the rather unpleasant subject-matter. An unmarried mother gives birth to a child (twins in some variants). In despair she takes out her penknife (the ultimate weapon in balladry) and murders the child. Living to regret this terrible crime, she is walking to church one day when she is moved by the sight of a child. Thereafter the following exchange:

> 'O sweet babe, and thou were mine,
> I wad clad thee in the silk so fine.'

> 'O mother dear, when I was thine,
> You did na prove to me sae kind.'

Occasionally revenants are kind. A rich woman, 'The Wife of Usher's Well' (79A), inadvertently sends her three sons to their death at sea. She is beside herself with grief. On Martinmas ('When nights are lang and mirk') the three sons return as revenants to comfort their mother. They wear birch hats ('their hats were o the birk') and are bound to leave before daylight in order to escape damnation. Still, the mother is ecstatic at seeing them again. As they depart, one of the brothers delivers a parting message which includes his sweetheart as well as his mother:

> 'Fare ye weel, my mother dear!
> Fareweel to barn and byre!
> And fare ye weel, the bonny lass
> That kindles my mother's fire!'

Child included 'The Suffolk Miracle' (272) in his book because 'in a blurred, enfeebled, and disfigured shape, it is the representative in England of one of the most impressive and beautiful ballads of the European continent'. A farmer forbids his daughter to see her loved one; unknown to her the young man pines away and dies. After a month he comes to her, as a revenant, and she gives him a handkerchief to tie round his head when he complains of a headache. This visit causes consternation all round. The young man's grave is opened and there, round the head of the rotting corpse, is the handkerchief. Love, apparently, conquers all. Yet a warning against excessive mourning for a lost true-love is sounded in 'The Unquiet Grave' (78A). A young man vows to mourn his dead lover for 'a twelvemonth and a day'. This is acceptable in the ballad world. When the period is exceeded the corpse speaks, complaining that she cannot rest because of his terrible morbidity:

> 'You crave one kiss of my clay-cold lips;
> But my breath smells earthy strong;
> If you have one kiss of my clay-cold lips,
> Your time will not be long.
>
> 'Tis down in younder garden green,
> Love, where we used to walk,
> The finest flower that ere was seen
> Is withered to a stalk.'

Some of the magical and supernatural glimpses given by the ballads are pleasant, some bizarre. More of a caricature than a character is the hideous lady: in 'The Marriage of Sir Gawain' (31) and 'King Henry' (32) the hideous lady is reassuringly transformed into a beauty: in 'Allison Gross' (35) and 'The Laily Worm and the Machrel of the Sea' (36) the hideous lady has become a witch who changes her adversaries into loathsome serpents. Just as mortals outwit the devil in the riddling ballads, so they outwit witches in the supernatural ballads. Witchcraft may be present as a folklore element but it is always vulnerable, which shows the folk were not at the mercy of mindless superstition.

One of the great ballads taken down from the recitation of Mrs Brown of Falkland, 'Willie's Lady' (6A), deals with a mortal triumph over witchcraft. Willie has married a beautiful golden-haired woman who is now pregnant but unable to give birth. This is because Willie's mother, a witch, has cast a spell over the young girl. When Willie offers the maternal witch three gifts of gold to remove the spell, she answers each time:

> 'But she shall die and turn to clay,
> And ye shall wed another may.'

Thanks to the assistance of the Billy Blin, the household familiar, a plot is hatched against Willie's mother whereby Willie models a glass-eyed waxen child and invites his mother to the christening. Thinking her spell has been broken, the old woman reveals all the details of it; it is then a simple matter for Willie to undo the spell and allow his wife to give birth to 'a bonny young son'.

Magic, the perpetual presence of impossibility, is a rich narrative source of balladry. In the ballad world things happen suddenly and without warning; the fatal powers of destruction can be overcome by the help of magic. Thomas of Erceldoun, the venerated prophetic poet of Scotland, acquires his powers after a seven-year stretch in elfland. In 'Thomas Rymer' (37A) the poet is enchanted by the queen of elfland and 'till seven years were past and gone / True Thomas on earth was never seen'. Another person privileged to look into the secrets of elfland is 'The Wee Wee Man' (38A) and the fairy-folk turn out to be beautiful celebrants of beauty.

A great and heroic contest between human and fairy forces occurs in the superb Scottish ballad 'Tam Lin' (39A) which was communicated to James Johnson's *The Scots Musical Museum* (1787-1803) by Robert Burns. Despite warnings about the dangers to her maidenhead in Carterhaugh, the fearless Janet goes there and is seduced by Tam. Although her friends are shocked at Janet's pregnancy she is proud of bearing a child to such a man:

> 'The steed that my true-love rides on
>> Is lighter than the wind;
> Wi siller he is shod before,
>> Wi burning gowd behind.'

In addition to her pride she has the courage of her convictions and is determined to rescue Tam from the fairy-folk who have captured him. He explains that at Hallowe'en she can have him if she holds on to him. She will recognize him by his milk-white steed but will have to face some terrifying metamorphoses. Tam explains:

> 'They'll turn me to a bear sae grim,
>> And then a lion bold;
> But hold me fast, and fear me not,
>> As ye shall love your child.

> 'Again they'll turn me in your arms
>> To a red het gaud of airn [bar of iron];
> But hold me fast, and fear me not,
>> I'll do to you nae harm.

> 'And last they'll turn me in your arms
>> Into the burning gleed [coal];
> Then throw me into well water,
>> O throw me in wi speed.

> 'And then I'll be your ain true-love,
>> I'll turn a naked knight;
> Then cover me wi your green mantle,
>> And cover me out o sight.'

Janet, as might be expected, is magnificently equal to the task, much to the chagrin of the Queen of Fairies.

Those metamorphoses described in 'Tam Lin' (39A) indicate the sort of magical transformation enjoyed by the folk. A ballad of quite singular beauty, involving a metamorphosis, is

'The Great Silkie of Sule Skerry' (113). Child's version is in seven quatrains and is impressive; but an infinitely finer version was recorded by Professor Otto Anderson of Finland in 1938 from John Sinclair of Flotta, Orkney; the text of this is given in Bronson *(The Traditional Tunes of the Child Ballads,* Vol. II, pp. 564-5). Sule Skerry is an islet twenty-five miles west of Hoy Head in Orkney, and it was from there that the selkie (seal) came to change into human form and father a child on a nurse. When the nurse sits lullabying the child, speculating on the identity of its father, the selkie comes to explain his metamorphic nature in one of the most hauntingly beautiful quatrains in balladry:

> 'I am a man upon the land,
> I am a selchie in the sea,
> an' whin I'm far from every strand,
> my dwelling is in Shool Skerry.'

The outcome of this ballad is that the child becomes a seal, joins his father in the sea, and both of them are shot by a gunner. The nurse knows her selkie-son by the gold chain she has placed around his neck and she ends lamenting:

> 'Alas, alas, this woeful fate,
> this weary fate, that's been laid on me.'
> An' ance or twice she sobbed and sighed,
> an' her tender heart did brak in three.

That such a magnificent ballad could still be in oral circulation in 1938 shows, more than anything else, the hold ballads have on the popular imagination.

Naturally the popular imagination was attracted to stories that had the raw presence of human destiny rather than the cluttered details of national history. Life was determined by an intractable environment to which folk fatally succumbed. When nature decided to impose itself on individuals it had all the elemental force of fire, air, earth and water.

Of all the sea ballads the best-known (certainly in Scotland where it is one of those things every schoolboy knows) is 'Sir Patrick Spens' (58A). Many people, when they think of a ballad, think of this one: the image that comes to mind is of the king sitting in Dunfermline drinking his blood-red wine. It is a great ballad that derives most of its power from counterpoint. The king's wine is contrasted with the water swallowed by the sailors he sends to the sea, and the reaction of Sir Patrick to the royal summons is conveyed by juxtaposition:

> The first line that Sir Patrick red,
> A loud lauch lauched he;
> The next line that Sir Patrick red,
> The teir blinded his ee.

After the tragic drowning of Sir Patrick and his crew — tragic because avoidable: it was the wrong 'time o' the yeir' — the magnitude of the disaster is established in a vivid set of contrasting images. The reluctance of the Scottish nobles to wet their feet is counterpointed against the description of their bodies sinking underneath their hats; the image of men lost at sea is counterpointed against the elegant ladies safe on shore:

> O our Scots nobles wer richt laith
> To weet their cork-heild schoone;
> Bot lang owre a' the play wer played,
> Their hats they swam aboone.

> O lang, lang may their ladies sit,
> Wi their fans into their hand,
> Or eir they se Sir Patrick Spence
> Cum sailing to the land.

It has been suggested that 'Sir Patrick Spens' (58) is historically based; Motherwell supposed the drowning to be connected with the return voyage to Scotland of Alexander III's daughter after her marriage in 1281 to Eric, King of Norway. Historical accuracy, however, is largely irrelevant to balladry;

a good ballad has a poetic independence unthreatened by historical fact. Thus the reality or otherwise of Robin Hood is not at issue when we consider the Robin Hood sequence of ballads (Child Nos 117-54), the most cohesive thematic group in Child. Robin Hood is the only character who appears in a large number of ballads and this because he was the darling of the minstrels. Popular ballads elevate action above characterization; minstrel ballads of Robin Hood depended on their principal character. In Robin Hood the minstrels knew they had a winner; his name was enough to sell a song. Basically Robin is a simple soul: he is piously devoted to Our Lady, he loves individual combat (though he frequently loses), he is more than a match for his greatest opponent the Sheriff of Nottingham. In short, Robin is 'a gode yeoman', as we are constantly reminded in the ballads.

In the thirty-eight ballads that comprise the Robin Hood sequence the good yeoman assumes disguises and picks fights, steals the king's deer but honours the king himself, abuses the clergy but respects the poor. He is the outlaw with the heart of gold. The Robin Hood legend has been extant at least since the fourteenth century, for Sloth, in *Piers Plowman,* mentions 'rymes of Robyn Hood'. This mention of 'rymes' supports the general view that few Robin Hood ballads were ever sung: the industrious Bronson admits that 'The record of tunes for the Robin Hood ballads is disappointingly meagre and uncertain' (*The Traditional Tunes of the Child Ballads*, Vol. III, p. 13). 'Robin Hood and the Monk' (119) ends:

> Thus endys the talkyng of the munke
> And Robyn Hode i-wysse

which implies recitation rather than singing. However, if these minstrel ballads were not popular in Child's sense of being narrative songs in oral circulation, they certainly created a popular hero. As Child says in his headnotes to 'A Gest of Robyn Hode' (117), 'Robin Hood is absolutely a creation of the ballad-muse'.

The 'Gest' (117) is the most sustained presentation of the good yeoman; it is a popular epic made from several ballads and amounting to 456 quatrains. The plot concerns Robin's magnanimity to the poor knight Sir Richard at the Lee, his slaying of the iniquitous Sheriff of Nottingham, and his reconciliation with authority in the shape of his beloved king. Robin is portrayed as a model of chivalry, and his death is greatly lamented:

> Cryst have mercy on his soule,
> That dyed on the rode!
> For he was a good outlawe,
> And dyde pore men moch god.

In the Robin Hood sequence there are some great individual ballads such as 'Robin Hood and the Monk' (119) in which, thanks to Little John, Robin escapes from the dreaded Sheriff, but as the sequence goes on the quality declines and it ends with a glib Martin Parker broadside. As Child said, also in his headnotes to the 'Gest' (117), 'A considerable part of the Robin Hood poetry looks like char-work done for the petty press, and should be judged as such.'

Immediately after the Robin Hood ballads Child assembled a group of historical, semi-historical and pseudo-historical ballads (Nos 154-242), a group that includes the Border ballads. First in this historically orientated group is 'Sir Hugh, or, The Jew's Daughter' (155A). which alludes to Hugh of Lincoln whose murder by Jews is told in an entry for 1255 in the *Annals of the Monastery of Waverley*. In the ballad Sir Hugh, after kicking a football through the 'Jew's window', is enticed into the Jew's castle and murdered by the Jew's daughter. His corpse miraculously directs his mother to the scene of the crime. Abandoning his scholarly impartiality, Child vehemently delivered himself of a personal opinion in his headnote to 'Sir Hugh' (155A). Child introduced the subject of antisemitism, pointed out that 'Murders like that of Hugh of Lincoln have been imputed to the Jews for at least seven hundred and fifty years', and concluded:

> . . . these pretended child-murders, with their horrible conse-
> quences, are only a part of a persecution which, with all
> moderation, may be rubricated as the most disgraceful chap-
> ter in the history of the human race.

If 'Sir Hugh' (155A) maliciously twists historical facts, then that is to be expected, for the folk took only what they wanted from history. They were interested in edification, not documen-tation, and real people were only grist to the ballad-singer's mill. For example, we know that twelve days after giving birth to Prince Edward on 12 October 1537 Jane Seymour died. 'The Death of Queen Jane' (170B) substitutes melodrama for his-tory; here the delivery is erroneously supposed to have been a Caesarian operation, the complications of which kill the queen:

But with sighing and sobbing she's fallen in a swoon,
Her side it was ript up, and her babie was found;
At this bonie babie's christning there was meikle joy and mirth,
But bonnie Queen Jeanie lies cold in the earth.

It is often the case that the more distorted the history the bet-ter the ballad. 'Earl Bothwell' (174), which quite convincingly attributes the murder of Darnley to Bothwell as a Mary-inspired reprisal for the murder of Riccio, is a lifeless affair. On the other hand 'The Bonny Earl of Murray' (181A) starts from the historical murder of the earl on 7 February 1592 and gains its strength from the purely fictional conjecture that the earl was a lover of James VI's queen:

He was a braw gallant,
    And he playd at the glove;
And the bonny Earl of Murray,
    Oh he was the Queen's love!

Again, 'Mary Hamilton' (173A) is about a real character, one of the four maries (maids) of Mary Queen of Scots. In the ballad Mary Hamilton is executed because she has murdered the child she had by Darnley, 'the hichest Stewart of a' '. There is no factual foundation for this whatsoever, though no doubt the folk were willing to believe anything about the debauched Darnley. This corruption of history has given us one of the most frequently quoted quatrains in balladry:

> 'Last nicht there was four Maries,
> The nicht there'll be but three;
> There was Marie Seton, and Marie Beton,
> And Marie Carmichael and me.'

Undoubtedly the most widely discussed historical ballad is 'Chevy Chase' — 'The Hunting of the Cheviot' (162B) — and this brings us to the Border territory. Three ballads deal with the battle fought on 19 August 1388 between the Scots under the Earl of Douglas and the English under Henry Percy. The Scots lost Douglas, but the English lost the battle and Percy was captured. 'The Battle of Otterburn' (161A) gives quite an accurate picture of the battle:

> Thys fraye bygan at Otterborne,
> Bytwene the nyght and the day;
> Ther the Dowglas lost hys lyffe,
> And the Perssy was lede awaye.

In the C version, which appeared in Scott's *Minstrelsy,* Douglas has taken on more tragic proportions and has an ominous dream about his posthumous victory:

> 'But I have dreamed a dreary dream,
> Beyond the Isle of Sky;
> I saw a dead man win a fight,
> And I think that man was I.'

'The Hunting of the Cheviot' (162A) distorts history by having Percy, as well as Douglas, killed; the B text, the famous 'Chevy

Chase', is a broadside version of the A text, so again both antagonists are slain:

> Thus did both those nobles dye,
> whose courage none cold staine;

History, in the ballads, provides only raw material for rousing narratives.

Ever since the immense success of Scott's *Minstrelsy*, Border has seemed almost the essential epithet of ballad so that you can't have one without the other. In fact the Border ballads make up only a small proportion of the Child canon, and, despite Scott, the richest area of balladry has been the Scottish north-east rather than the Scottish Border. Still, it has to be admitted that the Border ballads are in a class of their own. The recklessness of the characters, the vicious to-ing and fro-ing across the Border, the examples of heroism — these qualities make the Border ballads supremely exciting examples of popular art.

The rule of lawlessness in Border life is seen to perfection in 'Johnie Armstrong' (169A). The historical basis for this is that in 1530 James V levied an army of around 12,000 men to pacify the Borders. In this campaign Johnie Armstrong was killed. In the ballad James V summons Johnie to Edinburgh with a promise of safe conduct. When Johnie reaches the capital he is told he is to be hanged. In true Border style he refuses to accept this lying down and fights ferociously for his life before being stabbed in the back. Though long since dead, Johnie is a Border immortal, a man animated by pride and arrogance:

> He had nither lands nor rents coming in,
> Yet he kept eight score men in his hall.

Another Johnny Armstrong appears in 'Dick o the Cow' (185). After taking part in a cattle-raid on Dick o the Cow, 'an innocent fool' who lives near Carlisle, Johnny makes off with the goods. In hot pursuit comes Dick who manages to outwit the Armstrongs, beat Johnny in single combat, and sell two

Armstrong horses. Fool though he is, Dick is wise enough to move far away from Armstrong territory. Some of the tales of rescue are great sustained performances — like 'Kinmont Willie' (186) in which the Duke of Buccleuch rescues Kinmont Willie Armstrong from Carlisle Castle, or 'Jock o the Side' (187A). The latter was judged by Child to be 'one of the best in the world, and enough to make a horse-trooper of any young borderer, had he lacked the impulse'.

Jock, yet another Armstrong, has been taken prisoner to Newcastle; Hobby Noble says he will rescue him with five men. They manage to spring Jock but, as his feet are chained, he has to ride like a bride — to Hobby Noble's amusement. 'Archie of Cawfield' (188) is virtually a variant of 'Jock o the Side' (187A) but with Halls taking the place of Armstrongs. 'Hobie Noble' (189) recalls the hero of 'Jock o' the Side' (187A) to the stage. Hobie is betrayed and taken to Carlisle where he is recognized as 'the man loosd Jock o the Side'. Nobly, Hobie refuses food, saying he would rather die as Hobie Noble than live as a traitor. He takes his leave with a defiant Last Goodnight.

Two of the Border ballads refer to Yarrow, the Scottish river which flows into the Tweed. 'The Braes of Yarrow' (214A) begins with an ominous dream as a lady thinks she sees her husband 'come headless hame'. In spite of this the husband goes to meet his brother-in-law on the braes of Yarrow; there he is ambushed and killed from behind. The brother-in-law callously tells his sister that her husband is 'sleeping sound on Yarrow', so she goes to him, combs his hair, ties her own yellow hair around her neck and kills herself on Yarrow. 'Rare Willie Drowned in Yarrow' (215A) is a short lyrical piece in which a lady, looking forward to her wedding, finds her man drowned in the river:

> She sought him east, she sought him west,
>> She sought him brade and narrow;
> Sine, in the clifting of a craig,
>> She found him drownd in Yarrow.

Towards the end of his collection Child gathered together a number of comic ballads (Child Nos 273-8); with the splendid exception of 'Get Up and Bar the Door' (275A) these are not of the highest order of balladry. The reduction of a superlative narrative song to a comical musical ditty is an egregious collapse of standards. The ballad worked best when the narrative/musical package was delivered to folk who were seriously receptive to its contents. For them the narrative medium was the message. They wanted to be told stories that would enrich their lives, that would give them something to sing about or lament over. Some of them would, in turn, pass the package on with embellishments here and there, and so the stories travelled, acquiring local variants on the journey. But always there was a point to the story, something that engaged the attention in a worthy manner. The ballads mattered to the ballad people.

This is a crucial point about the ballads. They were not conceived in splendid artistic isolation to gratify the inspirational genius of a lonely creator. They were made to be used, to be handed on. They have the strength of solid workmanship about them. If they were to impress people who lived by the labour of their hands then they had to show utterly lasting qualities. The local ballad-singer was not a full-time poet but an integral part of the community with a special gift for retaining and, in some cases, improving stories that were passed from generation to generation. The ballads were the proud possession of people who were obsessed by survival and wanted their entertainment to survive with them. The structural solidity of the ballads is a tribute to the staying power of the folk.

I have evoked the image of the ballad as a sturdy package. It came with recognizable stylistic wrappings and the contents were something to retain, to cherish. When we consider the condition of the ballad folk we consider people who could not live by bread alone but wanted, at times, to be wrapped in the seamless garment of great art. This is what the ballad package contained.

Ballads are stories tailored for popular usage rather than for aesthetic display; the folk who made use of them tested them for durability and discarded the parts that didn't fit their needs. Hence the concision of the ballads as they have come down to us. They are strong yarns worn down to the bare essentials. The popular demand for good stories was obviously immense, and in considering the contents of balladry I have attempted to suggest how certain narrative threads proved more attractive than others.

4

The broadside ballads

The vulgar ballads of our day, the 'broadsides' which were
printed in such large numbers in England and elsewhere in the
sixteenth century or later ... are products of a low kind of *art*,
and most of them are, from a literary point of view, thoroughly
despicable and worthless.

(Francis James Child, Appendix to 1965 reprint of
The English and Scottish Popular Ballads, p. 757)

Technically, a broadside is an unfolded sheet printed on one
side; artistically, however, the term has acquired a pejorative
meaning. Because so many traditional ballads were issued in
the broadside format Child had to use these texts in his *magnum opus*. When he did so he was at pains to deprecate the
form. His headnote to 'The Hunting of the Cheviot' (162)
includes the comment that the most familiar version, 'Chevy
Chase' (162B) — the one praised by Addison — 'is a striking
but by no means a solitary example of the impairment which
an old ballad would suffer when written over for the broadside
press'. So, in addition to its existence as a bibliographical arte-
fact, the broadside ballad has had to carry critically unpleasant
connotations. It is easy to see why. Whereas popular ballads
were, ideally, transmitted orally, broadsides were hastily
issued for commercial gain; whereas popular ballads were the
work of anonymous amateurs, broadsides were usually the
work of hacks; whereas popular ballads were timeless, broadsides were topical; whereas popular ballads were largely rural
entertainments, broadsides were eagerly devoured by the
urban masses — by the people Milton described as 'A miscel-

laneous rabble, who extol / Things vulgar' *(Paradise Regained,* III, 50-1).

The popular ballads, as we have seen, offer immense scope for scholarly speculation: the ambiguity of their origins has been a godsend to critics in search of a subject. The broadsides exist as tangible documents, as a crude means of exploiting the possibilities of the mass medium of printing. Caxton's *Recuyell of the Historyes of Troye,* the first English printed book, was produced at Bruges in 1475, and by 1500 around 360 books had been printed in England. The existence of cheap printing in the sixteenth century made possible the mass publication of broadsides. John Skelton's elegy on King Henry VII (*c.* 1509) is probably the earliest printed broadside, and the same poet's 'A Ballade of the Scottyshe Kynge' dates from 1513; a dialogue between 'Luther, the Pope, and a Husbandman' dates from *c.* 1535. Broadsides were easy to produce and easily accessible; once the format had been established, the market was flooded.

In the mid-sixteenth century broadside printers were legally obliged to register their ballads, and more than 3000 are listed for the period 1557-1709; many more would be unregistered. With their crude woodcut illustrations and accompanying verses, the broadsides were the metrical journalism of the masses. They were hawked on the streets and purchased, for a halfpenny or a penny, by seekers after sensation. They offered a diet of murder, deformity (the story of the unfortunate pig-faced lady was current from 1639 to 1815), gossip and news. They were a lucrative source of income for the publishers and a source of delight to those who bought them.

The interest in broadsides was not confined to the 'miscellaneous rabble'. Indeed, were it not for the fascination exerted by the broadsides on highly educated men, we would not now be in a position to study the genre. Samuel Pepys, basing his collection on the horde amassed by the scholar John Selden, possessed 1671 separate street ballads. His thematic arrangement of them in five volumes under ten headings gives an excellent summary of the subject-matter covered by the broadside press:

1 Devotion and Morality. 2 History — True and Fabulous. 3 Tragedy - viz. Murd[ers] Execut[ions] Judgm[ents] of God. 4 State and Times. 5 Love — Pleasant. 6 do [i.e. Love] — Unfortunate. 7 Marriage, Cuckoldry, &c. 8 Sea — Love, Gallantry, & Actions. 9 Drinking & Good Fellowship. 10 Humour, Frollicks, &c. mixt.

Pepys gifted his collection to Magdalene College, Cambridge, where it now comprises part of the Pepysian Library. Pepys had completed his collection by 1703, but before that another lover of broadsides, Anthony Wood (1632-95), had accumulated a huge number of broadsides. Because of the indiscriminate plunder of his papers, only 279 ballads remain in the Wood Collection at the Bodleian Library, Oxford. Many ballads collected by Wood eventually helped make up the Rawlinson Collection (218 ballads at the Bodleian) and the Roxburghe Collection (almost 1500 ballads at the British Museum).

As the makers and sellers of street ballads came into contact with a large popular market, they often fell foul of the authorities, who felt they had a duty to control public opinion. An Act for the Advancement of True Religion, passed by Parliament in 1543, cites the theologically subversive influence of 'printed ballads, rhymes and songs' and required booksellers to provide lists of their ballads. Shortly after the coronation, in 1553, of 'Bloody Mary' Tudor, a royal proclamation condemned the printing of 'books, ballads, rhymes and interludes': in fact, printers of heretical ballads were persecuted while Catholics like John Heywood printed ecclesiastically acceptable ballads with impunity. When Elizabeth I became queen in 1558 this policy was reversed so that the Catholic ballad-writers had to go underground.

The Elizabethan age was incredibly rich in street ballads — in 1569-70 Stationers' Hall licensed 100 of them. Though the likes of Shakespeare (see Autolycus in *The Winter's Tale*) and Johnson (see Nightingale in *Bartholomew Fair)* held the ballad-mongers up to ridicule, nothing could stem the broadside tide. William Elderton was a prolific and accomplished broadside writer who, in 1571, was censured by the Privy Council for writing ballads 'to the discreditt of some presences with whom the Queen Ma[jes] tie standeth presently in terms of amytie'. Elderton was succeeded as the foremost broadside balladeer by Thomas Deloney from whose *The Garland of Good-Will* (registered 1593) we derive the term 'garland' for a collection of broadsides (though actually the first of the garlands was Clement Robinson's *Handful of Pleasant Delights* of 1566). Elderton and Deloney were competent practitioners. When the Earl of Essex's expedition of June/July 1596 — an expedition in which John Donne took part — captured and sacked Cadiz, Deloney was ready with his ballad 'The Winning of Cales' (Cales being the Elizabethan form of Cadiz):

> Long the proud Spaniard
>   advanced to conquer us,
> Threatning our Country
>   with fire and sword,
> Often preparing
>   their Navy most sumptuous,
> With all the provision
>   that *Spain* could afford,
> Dub, a dub, dub,
>   thus strikes their Drummes,
> Tan ta ra ra, tan ta ra ra,
>   English men comes.

These lines are admirable for their vigour, their defiantly strutting rhythm, their metrical competence: generalizations that condemn all broadsides as doggerel foolishly ignore the idiomatic expertise of a man like Deloney.

The publication of a broadside meant instant fame for a person or event. No wonder that Sir John Falstaff, in demanding recognition of his fancied victory over the rebel leader Sir John Colville, insisted (*2 Henry IV,* IV. iii) that his feat 'be booked with the rest of this day's deed; or, by the Lord, I will have it in a particular ballad else, with mine own picture on the top of it'. Falstaff might have been disappointed with his 'own picture', for it would likely have been a likeness of someone else. With their indifferent draughtsmanship and lack of compositional clarity, the woodcut illustrations on broadsides were an accurate pictorial counterpart of the verse. Both were two-dimensional with no illusion of depth. The woodcuts were used again and again and their all-purpose versatility meant that one woodcut could illustrate dozens of different ballads. Shepard (*The History of Street Literature,* pp. 160-1) reproduces two broadsides which use the identical woodcut of a hirsute, vaguely aristocratic gentleman. In the blackletter (gothic type) broadside, 'Opportunity Lost', he is a 'Scotch lover'; in a Pitts whiteletter (roman type) reprint of 'Lord Thomas and Fair Eleanor' (73D) he is Lord Thomas. Pitts had acquired the woodcut and used it whenever it was remotely appropriate. Henry Mayhew, chronicling mid-nineteenth century London, was told by an informant: ' "Here you have also an exact likeness", they say, "of the murderer, taken at the bar of the Old Bailey!" when all the time it is an old wood-cut that's been used for every criminal for the last forty years' (see Shepard, *The History of Street Literature,* p. 101). The pictorial content of the ballads, then, was as feeble as much of the verse.

Despite many attempts to supress them, the street ballads retained their popularity and positively flourished in the seventeenth century, even when Cromwellian and then Restoration censorship meant that politically unacceptable ballads had to settle for an illegal existence. The drama of the Civil War, the Commonwealth and the Restoration provided a superfluity of subjects for the broadside writers; one of them produced a lively satire on 'The Lancashire Puritan':

> He killd his Catt (as most men say)
> For mousing on the Sabboath day;
> And *Hunt* his Hound did the Gallows clime
> For Sleeping in the Sermon time:
>   Hee loaths the Flesh but loves the Sprite,
> Hee's *Purus-putus* Hypocrite.

The evidence of street balladry was everywhere — since they were printed only on the recto, they could be pasted up on the walls of private and public houses. In the second chapter of *The Compleat Angler* (1653) Izaak Walton mentions 'an honest ale-house, where we shall find a cleanly room, lavendar in the windows, and twenty ballads stuck about the wall'. The great broadside balladeer of the seventeenth century was Martin Parker, author of the royalist 'When the king enjoys his own again'. Parker, who headed a syndicate of more than twenty broadside writers, was adept at satisfying the demand for incredible occurrences. His 'A Description of a Strange (and Miraculous) Fish' (*c.* 1635) shows his talent for exaggeration:

> Full twenty one yards and one foot
>   this fish extends in length,
> With all things correspondent too't,
>   for amplitude and strength:
> Good people what I shall report,
> Doe not account it fained sport.
>   *O rare*
>   *beyond compare,*
> *in England nere the like.*

Parker's insistence on the veracity of his story is characteristic of the street ballad. What was being offered to the public was not to be thought of as mere gossip but as hard fact: the authority of print reinforced this fiction. The final entry in Child's long sequence of Robin Hood ballads is a broadside, Martin Parker's 'A True Tale of Robin Hood' (154); in this instance, too Parker is adamant about his own reliability:

> I know there's many fained tales
> Of Robbin Hood and 's crew;
> But chronicles, which seldom fayles,
> Reports this to be true.

The public's belief in the inviolability of the printed word meant that the broadsides fixed texts; once a traditional ballad appeared in broadside it tended to become fossilized. There was simply no need for the public to rely on oral performers.

Often the impact of print on the public mind had political repercussions, as was the case with the Marquis of Wharton's 'Lilliburlero' (1688) which contributed to the downfall of James II. It became tremendously popular, the unofficial anthem of the Glorious Revolution. It purports to report a conversation between two Irishmen who are exulting over the imminent victory of popery:

> And he dat will not go to Mass,
> Li-li Burlero Bullen a-la,
> Shall turn out and look like an Ass,
> Li-li Bur-le-ro Bullen a la,
> Le-ro, Le-ro, Le-ro, Le-ro, Li-li Bur-le-ro, Bullen a-la,
> Le-ro, Le-ro, Le-ro, Le-ro, Li-li Bur-le-ro, Bullen a-la.

To reach the public, the ballad-writers and printers had to rely on chapmen and patterers. These characters are an essential part of the whole broadside phenomenon. A chapbook — or cheapbook — was a pamphlet made from a sheet folded into four, eight, twelve or sixteen uncut, uncovered and unstitched pages. Chapbook collections of ballads were, as we have seen, known as garlands. The chapmen who sold these products — on which they got one-third discount — had to be colourful enough to attract attention to themselves and their wares. One of the most colourful of all was Dougal Graham. Born in the village of Raploch, near Stirling, in 1724, Dougal began life as a farm worker but was 'out' with Bonnie Prince Charlie in the '45 Rebellion. After the disaster of Culloden he published his own *History of the Rebellion* in 5000 rhymed lines and sold it for fourpence. (By 1828, long after Dougal's death, it had gone through twenty editions.) Dougal Graham travelled the Scottish lowlands selling his stock, a large proportion of which was all his own work, like the autobiographical *John Cheap the Chapman.* He earned enough to establish his own printing office in Glasgow's Saltmarket and in 1772, thanks to his rapid line in patter, he was elected Skellat Bellman (town crier) of the city of Glasgow at an annual salary of £10. He died around 1779.

It is somewhat ironic that it was only after their popular decline that ballads — both oral and broadside — acquired respectability. Men like Dougal Graham were, socially, polar opposites of the modern ballad scholar. Ballads were always associated with a low standard of living. We know that Addison and Percy had to apologize for their interest in the simple ballads of the common people; the street ballads, being on a much lower level, have taken that much longer to attract scholarly attention. While the broadside ballad existed as an inescapable part of urban life it had a disreputable name; the men who made the broadsides were regarded as culturally unspeakable and completely mercenary. Those who went out on the streets and sold the ballads were offensive to polite society. The attitude of official Birmingham in 1794 is fairly typical: 'The Officers of this Town give this public Notice, that they are come to a determined Resolution to apprehend all strolling Beggars, Ballad Singers, and other Vagrants found within this Parish' (Palmer, *A Touch on the Times,* p. 13).

Street balladry, then, was classed with vagrancy. The half-penny and penny broadside ballads were sold by patterers. They would speak and sing their wares with emphasis on the most sensational details. The standing patterer, working from a fixed pitch marked by a pictorial board, performed many of his ballads to attract passers-by. The running patterer kept on the move, pursuing customers by giving a running commentary on his stock. In his *London Labour and the London Poor* (1851) Henry Mayhew wrote of the frantic efforts of the patterers to sell their wares:

> It is not possible to ascertain with any certitude *what* the patterers are so anxious to sell, for only a few leading words are audible. One of the cleverest of the running patterers repeated to me, in a subdued tone, his announcements of murders. The words 'Murder', 'Horrible', 'Barbarous', 'Love', 'Mysterious', 'Former Crimes', and the like, could only be caught by the ear, but there was no announcement of anything like 'particulars'.... The running patterers describe, or profess to describe, the contents of their papers as they go rapidly along, and they seldom or ever stand still.
>
> (Shepard, *The History of Street Literature,* p. 72)

As well as the frenetic patterers there were the pinners-up who would display ballads along a wall or set of railings. The mind of lower London belonged to these men.

Thanks to the stamp duty imposed on newspapers, the patterers and pinners-up had a near-monopoly of the popular market. The first genuine newspaper, *The London Gazette,* appeared as a half-sheet printed on both sides in 1665, but the prohibitive duty restricted the sale of newspapers to the reasonably affluent. In 1712 this duty was a penny per sheet and by 1815 it had increased to fourpence. This, combined with poor distribution, put the newspapers at a disadvantage. The printers of street literature gleefully pandered to the market they had virtually to themselves.

In the nineteenth century there was a tremendous revival of the broadside press, particularly in London's slummy Seven Dials district inhabited by Irish immigrants, beggars, criminals and lowlifers: it had been, appropriately, the setting for John Gay's *The Beggar's Opera* (1728). In 1802 John Pitts (1765-1844), the son of a baker, set up a printing business at 14 Great St Andrew Street, Seven Dials, and in 1819 moved to 6 Great St Andrew Street, with his Toy and Marble Warehouse. Pitts found the publication of halfpenny ballads a steady source of income, and his stock included traditional ballads like 'Lord Thomas and Fair Eleanor' (73D) as well as folksongs and ballads collected from the Irish immigrants. Pitts invented the long song-sheet of 'Three Yards a Penny', so called because though the sheet was about one yard long the three columns on it could be said to amount to three yards of print. Pitts eventually went blind, but this disability did nothing to impair his business acumen; what really encroached on him was the rivalry of James Catnach.

Catnach (1792-1841), the son of a Scottish printer, set up house and printing shop at 2 Monmouth Court, Seven Dials, in 1813. With a press that could initially produce 200 copies of a broadside per hour, he became the leading light of Seven Dials and soon eclipsed Pitts. He was a one-man industry: writing, printing and publishing his ballads. After the victory over Napoleon at Waterloo on 18 June 1815 Catnach produced his 'The Battle of Waterloo' which included the following lines, the sort of thing the urban masses lapped up:

Our Cavalry advanced with true and valiant hearts,
Our Infantry and Artillery did nobly play their parts,
While the small arms did rattle, and great guns did roar,
And many a valiant soldier bold lay bleeding in his gore.

A more tragic event of national importance occurred when, eighteen months after marrying Prince Leopold of Saxe-Coburg in 1816, Princess Charlotte — the only child of George

IV (then Regent during his father's madness) — died in child-birth. Catnach rose to the occasion with a verbal creak:

> She is gone with her joy — her darling Boy,
>> The son of Leopold blythe and keen;
> She Died the sixth of November,
>> Eighteen hundred and seventeen.

Shrewd businessman though he was, Catnach could over-step the mark — in 1819 he published an item on a local butcher Thomas Pizzey and went to jail on a charge of libel. Catnach's lurid publication told of 'a number of Human Bodies found in the shop of a Pork Butcher'; incensed by this malicious gossip some 200 people broke into Pizzey's shop and assaulted the butcher and his family. Catnach's imprisonment was too good an opportunity for Pitts to miss and he issued his own broadside comment on the matter:

> Now Jemmy Catnach's gone to prison,
>> And what's he gone to prison for?
> For printing a libel against Mr Pizzey,
>> Which was sung from door to door.

> Six months in quad old Jemmy got,
>> Because he a shocking tale had started,
> About Mr Pizzey who dealt in sausages
>> In Blackmore Street, Clare Market.

The fate of those who landed in prison for more serious crimes than Catnach's was of major interest to broadside balladeers. Soon they began to produce a species of broadside known as the Sorrowful Lamentation, a corruption of the Last Goodnight of the popular ballads. In 1820 the law decreed that there should be a decent hiatus between trial and execution, and this allowed the broadside writers to prepare a Sorrowful Lamentation for sale at the execution. Executions were public in Britain until 1866 and attracted some enormous crowds: in September 1849, for example, the murderer John Gleeson was hanged outside Liverpool's Kirkdale Jail before a crowd of 100,000 spectators. Catnach was able to turn out many monsterpieces in the Sorrowful Lamentation vein; one of them, a 'Lamentation and Confession of John William Holloway, who now lies in Horsham Gaol, awaiting his Trial for the Cruel Murder of his Wife', closed:

In these dark cells of Horsham gaol I cry both day and night,
    For the bleeding corpse of my poor wife is always in my sight:
When I hope her soul is in heaven at rest when I tormented I shall be,
    I deserve nothing but the Burning Flames for my sad cruelty.

Now young and old, pray beware of my unhappy fate,
    Pray let your Parsons comfort you before it is too late;
Hark! hark! I hear the dismal bell, how harsh it tolls —
    May the Lord have mercy on me and all poor unhappy souls!

It is hard to imagine more sorrowful verse than Catnach was capable of producing at his worst. It was symptomatic of his profession. Unlike the popular ballads, which slowly evolved by oral transmission, the broadsides were churned out as quickly as possible; people bought them for the packaged information, not for the poetry. Catnach was a terrible poet but an excellent businessman. In 1823 he made £500 by producing 250,000 copies of a broadside on the murder of William Weare by John Thurtell. It seems that the term 'catchpenny' to describe a deceptive publication was coined when, two weeks after Thurtell's execution on 9 January 1824, Catnach produced a sheet headlined 'WE ARE ALIVE AGAIN' with so little space between the first two words that the public thought the murdered man had returned from the dead.

Even more scandalous was the murder of Maria Marten at the Red Barn for which crime William Corder was executed outside Bury Gaol on 10 August 1828. Catnach sold over a million copies of a broadside, probably his own composition, which purported to be a ballad on the 'Murder of M. Marten by W. Corder'. In true broadside style it piles horror on horror, describing Maria's 'bleeding mangled body', the discovery by Maria's father of 'his daughter mingling with the dust', and the use of Maria's jawbone as evidence in court. It ends with a criminal's Last Goodnight, supposedly spoken by the murderer:

Adieu, adieu, my loving friends, my glass is almost run,
On Monday next will be my last, when I am to be hang'd.
So you, young man, who do pass by, with pity look on me,
For murdering Maria Marten, I was hang'd upon the tree.

Almost anything of a sensational nature could expect to be celebrated in a broadside; the more sensational the better from the point of view of the public. Thus the ninety-three round, illegal, bare-fisted prizefight between Ben Caunt and William 'Bendigo' Thompson at Newport Pagnell on 9 September 1845 provoked, probably within a day, a broadside:

And near to Newport Pagnell,
Those men did strip so fine,
Ben Caunt stood six foot two and an half,
And Bendigo five foot nine,
Ben Caunt a giant did appear,
And made the claret flow,
And he seemed fully determined
Soon to conquer Bendigo.

Bendigo, however, was given a disputed decision. It was four years after that epic battle that Henry Mayhew first began to publish articles in the *Morning Chronicle* that would eventually appear as the two volumes of *London Labour and the London Poor* in 1851. Mayhew — attorney's son, dramatist and sometime co-editor of *Punch* — found London's streets teeming with all sorts of weird and wonderful creatures, including rat-killers, knife-swallowers, bug-destroyers and the urban ballad-singers. All had to use their wits to make a living, as Mayhew found when he talked with the street-patterers, the chaunters (who sang and fiddled), and the ballad-singers who sang for their suppers. London was full of ephemeral verse of the worst sort and the broadside was its repository.

The vigorous vulgarity of the broadside press continued throughout the nineteenth century. Wordworth's great autobiographical *Prelude* (completed by 1805) offered, when it was finally published in 1850, glimpses of London including

> Some half-frequented scene, where wider streets
> Bring straggling breezes of suburban air.
> Here files of ballads dangle from dead walls . . .
>
> (VII, 191-3)

An important fiscal decision was, in time, to remove the need for the writing on the walls. The abolition of stamp duty on newspapers in 1855 meant that the broadside press had to do open battle with a better-equipped, better-organized rival. *The Daily Telegraph,* which appeared in the wake of the abolition of stamp duty, was not typical of the journalistic shape of things to come, but by 1860 London had its *Evening Standard.* The real progenitor of the popular press, Alfred Charles William Harmsworth (Lord Northcliffe), revolutionized the newspaper industry by the creation of the *Daily Mail* in 1896 and the *Daily Mirror* in 1903. The broadside genesis of these popular newspapers was clearly revealed in the use of bold mastheads and provocative headlines, by the alliance of text and titillating pictorial matter, by the use of an eyecatching layout.

For a considerable while the broadside press and the popular press existed side by side. Henry Parker Such was in business from 1849 to 1917. From his premises at 124 Union Street, The Borough, in south-east London, he issued the usual diet of broadside monstrosities. One of his efforts (reproduced by Shepard, *The History of Street Literature*, p. 194) has the headline 'Murder at Cambridge' and a wordy subheading informing the reader that 'Robert Brown, stands charged with the murder of Emma Rolfe, by cutting her throat with a razor, on a Common near Cambridge, on Thursday night, Aug. 28th, 1876'. The ballad reinforces the message:

> She met with her murderer on Thursday night,
> They both went together soon after twilight;
> They went to the common for a purpose we know,
> They quarrelled and then he gave her a death blow;
> He then cut her throat with a razor so keen,
> The poor woman's blood on the pathway did stream.

It was the same mixture as before: functional verse, moralistic claptrap, sensation masquerading as moral outrage. Little wonder that the public came to prefer their sensation neat instead of having it filtered through a thick mesh of doggerel. Henry Parker Such ended up printing coloured handbills with the words of popular music-hall numbers.

Strangely enough, just as the broadside tradition was dying, the broadside muse was alive and well and living in Dundee: there lurked a self-styled genius who saw himself as a poet of Shakespearian dignity when all the time he was producing broadside material. William MacGonagall (1830–1902) might have been another Martin Parker in a broadside context; in a literary context, which is what he wanted for himself, he appears ludicrous. Compare Parker's poem on the miraculous fish (p. 71) with MacGonagall's infamous poem on 'The Famous Tay Whale' which begins:

> 'Twas in the month of December, and in the year 1883,
> That a monster whale came to Dundee,
> Resolved for a few days to sport and play,
> And devour small fishes in the silvery Tay.

and ends thirteen stanzas later:

> Then hurrah! for the mighty monster whale,
> Which has got 17 feet 4 inches from tip of a tail!

Which can be seen for a sixpence or a shilling,
That is to say, if the people all are willing.

MacGonagall has the real broadside style — forced rhymes, the inclusion of as much factual data as possible, and unbounded enthusiasm for his subject. It can be imagined what a Martin Parker or a Catnach would have given for such a natural command of bathos; instead MacGonagall missed his historical moment, his true vocation.

Although the broadsides were replaced by the popular press, the genre still exerts a fascination. Its unpretentious immediacy is especially attractive to poets who despair at the indifference of the public to poetry. They look back wistfully to a day when the public bought verse — of a kind — on the streets as casually as they might buy an apple. The broadside seems one way to reach the public. W. B. Yeats was particularly interested in broadsides. From a street ballad, 'The Rambling Boys of Pleasure', containing lines like

> Down by yon valley gardens,
> One evening as I chanced to stray . . .
> She told me to take love easy,
> Just as the leaves grow on the trees,
> But I being young and foolish,
> For then I did not agree.

he fashioned his beautiful 'Down by the Salley Gardens'. Yeat's younger sister, Elizabeth, founded the Dun Emer Press (later the Cuala Press) in 1903 and in July 1908 the press published the first of eighty-four numbers of *A Broadside*. It ran until 1916 — when a 'terrible beauty' was born — issuing traditional and modern ballads, some of which were illustrated by the poet's brother Jack B. Yeats.

Once a popular tradition dies there are always attempts to resuscitate it by a minority. The broadside, once a mass medium, is now in the custody of a cultured minority. Today, when poets find difficulty gaining access to commercial publishers, there is a revival of interest in the broadside; poems are issued in the broadside format and peddled, by the poets, in the pubs and on the streets. It is a peripheral activity undertaken by those who regard the broadside as a protected species. Sometimes the genuine broadside note is sounded; Ewan Mac-Coll, for example, issued a broadside about Timothy Evans who, in 1950, was executed for murders committed by John Christie in Rillington Place, London. It ended:

> They sent Tim Evans to the drop
> For a crime he didn't do.
> It was Christy was the murderer
> And the judge and jury too.

The general critical judgement of the broadside is that when the public buys verse in quantity it brings down the quality. I am not so sure. I feel that for too long too many literary people have remained aloof from popular culture as if contact with it would contaminate them. The lack of great broadside poetry says as much about the isolation of the sophisticated writer as it does about the 'miscellaneous rabble': the indifference of one to the other creates a cultural chasm that is too easily bridged by commerce. Meanwhile, as modern poetic broadsides appear in limited editions, the broadside spirit lives on in popular journalism. Without a shadow of doubt the old broadside press gave birth to the tabloids of today.

5

Survival of the ballads

> [The ballads] are extremely difficult to imitate by the highly civilised modern man, and most of the attempts to reproduce this kind of poetry have been ridiculous failures.
>
> (Francis James Child, Appendix to 1965 reprint of *The English and Scottish Popular Ballads*, p. 757)

When Child's great collection became a closed book, that did not signal the end of balladry. Though Child's industrious erudition had virtually completed the search for separate ballad stories, the tenacity of the popular tradition meant that new variants continued to be sung. In 1903 Cecil Sharp began to investigate the living traditions of Somerset and after four years' work he had recorded some 1500 tunes for ballads and folksongs. In the period 1904-14 Gavin Greig, a schoolteacher, discovered 107 variants of Child ballads current in the northeast of Scotland. Sharp then applied his astonishing energy to America and made three visits to the Appalachians in 1916, 1917 and 1918: in the course of a total of forty-six weeks of work he hand-notated 1612 tunes from almost 300 singers. With the slightly more advanced technological assistance of wax cylinders, Frank C. Brown began, in 1913, to search North Carolina and found tunes and textual variants for some fifty Child ballads; Phillips Barry did similarly useful work in New England. The quest for variants goes on with the handy aid of the modern tape recorder: the School of Scottish Studies in Edinburgh, inspired by the zeal of Hamish Henderson, has an archive that includes many variants of Child ballads.

The variants preserve the essential story, though some slight changes of emphasis are evident. In a version of 'Young Hunting' (68) collected by Sharp (see Bronson, *The Traditional Tunes of the Child Ballads,* Vol. II, p. 72) the pointlessness of Lady Margaret's jealous murder of her Love Henry is underlined by the talking bird:

> Up spoke, up spoke a pretty little parrot
> Exceeding on a willow tree:
> There never was a girl in Merry Green Lea
> He loved so well as thee.

In other words Love Henry was simply teasing his sweetheart. The most obvious thing that happens to ballads as they travel is the alteration of principal names. In Child the stonemason villain of 'Lamkin' (93) is also known as Balankin, Lamerlinkin, Rankin, Lambkin, Lord Lankyn, Long Lonkin, Bauld Rankin, Lanckin, Lord Longkin, Balcanqual, Lantin; Bronson's list of musical variants (ibid. Vol. II, pp. 428-45) supplies Bold Lantern, Bolakins, Beaulampkins, Squire Relantman, Bold Dunkins, Boab King and Bold Lankon. 'Lord Lovel' (75) similarly becomes Lord Lovat in Aberdeenshire because he could then be identified with a local hero of the '45 Rebellion.

The establishment of mass literacy and the publication of so many texts was bound to vitiate the oral tradition, for the singer now can learn ballads from a perusal of Child's texts and Bronson's tunes or from any one of hundreds of recordings. As Bronson points out (ibid. Vol. II, p. 321): 'Dissemination by phonograph and radio is a new kind of oral circulation, which is likely to have an effect on folk-tunes comparable to that of the broadside press on folk-texts.' No new ballads are likely to be created by the traditional oral method; and there is a limit to how much variation the ballad stories can stand. When British emigrants went in search of new worlds they carried their ballads with them. On new soil the songs took root, flourished and finally accepted the local cultural climate. Not always, though, with impressive effect. 'The Three Ravens' (26) has become, in American, a college song. The narrative content has vanished and instead we get:

> Said one old crow unto his mate,
>   'What shall we do for grub to ate?'
> And they all flapped their wings and cried,
>   'Caw! Caw! Caw! Billy Magee Magar!'
> And they all flapped their wings and cried,
>   'Billy Magee Magar!'

What Child — who thought the poignant 'The Twa Corbies' a 'cynical variation' of 'The Three Ravens' (26) — would have thought of such decadance can, fortunately, never be recorded.

What *is* impressive is the way the new countries eventually acquired ballads that are peculiarly their own. There were real-life outlaws like Ned Kelly (Australia) and Jesse James (USA) who fitted the Robin Hood mould. If Kelly and James had not existed, the folk would have had to invent them; in a sense they did by seeing them through a greenwood haze. They were clothed in the mantle of Robin Hood whose legend the folk would have brought over from England. Kelly (1854-80), the iron-plated terror of the Victoria / New South Wales border, was seen as a man more sinned against than sinning, a man forced into criminal life by an injustice against his mother. His exploit at Jerilderie in 1878, when he arrested the local police and dressed his gang in police uniform, duplicated Robin Hood's triumphs over the Sheriff of Nottingham. One of the members of the Kelly gang, Joe Byrne, celebrated the Jerilderie incident in a ballad that has since become public property in Australia:

> They rode into Jerilderie Town at twelve o'clock at night,
> They roused the troopers in their beds all in a dreadful
>   fright,
> They took them in their nightshirts, ashamed am I to tell,
> They covered them with revolvers and they locked
>   them in a cell.

Jesse James (1847-82) is, like Kelly, the subject of several ballads. His exploits as a bank robber, his betrayal by one of his own men, and above all the belief that

> He stole from the rich and he gave to the poor;
> He'd a hand and a heart and a brain.

were elements that combined to make Jesse the American Robin Hood. Some of the American ballads have acquired a global popularity that is unmatched by almost all the old traditional ballads. I would guess, for example, that more people today have heard the saga of 'Frankie and Johnny' than have heard the tale of Bonny Barbara Allan and her lovesick sweetheart. Black America too has its own ballad hero in 'John Henry', the mighty steel-driving man who worked the Chesapeake and Ohio's Big Band Tunnel in West Virginia in the early 1870s. A great modern folk hero, Muhammad Ali, composes his own ballads — orally, it would seem, though in the broadside tradition of inspired doggerel — to immortalize his achievements in the boxing ring. When he was still Cassius Clay and about to challenge Sonny Liston for the heavyweight championship of the world in 1964 he would address a mass audience, via television, and exclaim proleptically:

> Cassius throws out a left and connects with a right
> And the crowd sees the launching of the first coloured
>
> > satellite.
> Little did the people think when they put down their
>
> > money
> They were about to witness the total eclipse of the Sonny.

If orality has become almost redundant by the rise of mass literacy, then ballads still continue to come from literate sources. Once the individual composition of ballads has been accepted, it seems ludicrous to deny lettered poets the right to make their own ballads. These may not be accepted by the folk but they are still ballads in the sense of being strophic narratives, albeit *tuneless* strophic narratives. The individual creators of the traditional ballads were demonstrably great poets and their orality was imposed on them by social circumstances; literate poets can assert their individuality by fixing a text as and when they want. Ballad imitations represent perhaps the richest survival of balladry, a living poetic tradition. That tuneless literary ballads can have artistic validity is supported by the fact that for generations of readers — Child included — the text of a ballad was in itself sufficient. If a tuneless 'Sir Patrick Spens' (58) is not a ballad, then the term is deprived of all meaning.

In no small way Percy's *Reliques* were responsible for the Romantic revival of poetry in Britain. In his 1815 'Essay Supplementary to the Preface' Wordsworth felt that Britain's national poetry had been 'absolutely redeemed' by Percy's anthology: 'I do not think there is an able writer in verse of the present day who would not be proud to acknowledge his obligations to the *Reliques;* I know that it is so with my friends.' In 1800 Wordsworth and his friend Coleridge published, in two volumes, the second edition of their oxymoronically titled *Lyrical Ballads.* This edition, coming two years after the first, began with Wordsworth's Preface. Like Addison, who used the simplicity of the ballad style as a stick to beat Metaphysical poetry with, Wordsworth contrasted the 'artless' appeal of balladry with 'the gaudiness and inane phraseology of many modern writers'. To the cultivated poetic mind the ballad idiom was a call back to nature. Wordsworth's attempts to imitate the ballad showed that he was more familiar with broadside than traditional ballads. His 'Goody Blake and Harry Gill' has the dull ring of the typical broadside of the day:

> Old Goody Blake was old and poor;
> Ill fed she was, and thinly clad;
> And any man who passed her door
> Might see how poor a hut she had.

It was Coleridge, with 'The Rime of the Ancient Mariner', who seized on the traditional ballad as his model. Yet Coleridge was too self-consciously intellectual and philosophical to succumb to the spirit of the traditional ballad and his poem does not live up to its claim to have been 'written in imitation of the *style* as well as the spirit of the elder poets' (as the 'Advertisement' to the first edition of the *Lyrical Ballads* has it). The narrative bones of the story of the cursed mariner are made to rattle with an elaborate supernatural apparatus which is awkwardly attached to the poem. Many of the details are forced — the mariner's crossbow craftily becomes a portent of the cross symbol of the dead bird round his neck. There are abstractions like the pursuing Spirit and the vague figures of Death and Life-in-Death. There are deliberate archaisms — 'Eftsoons', 'Gramercy', 'countree', 'I trow', 'a-feared' — which sound like poor pastiche.

Coleridge's presence, as much as his poem, preceded what is probably the finest literary ballad. Keats's 'La Belle Dame Sans Merci' was included in a letter written to the poet's brother on 21 April 1819, ten days after Keats's meeting with Coleridge on Hampstead Heath. It splendidly simulates the impersonality of the ballad, being entirely written in dialogue — the three initial inquisitive quatrains being followed by the knight's nine-quatrain response. The figure of the knight was possibly taken from 'The Three Ravens' (26), though in the traditional ballad the knight is dead while in Keats's literary ballad the knight is 'Alone and palely loitering'. Some of the imagery was suggested by 'The Unquiet Grave' (78A). In that ballad the dead woman, weary of her lover's excessive mourning, delivers a *memento mori:*

> The finest flower that ere was seen
> Is withered to a stalk.

Keats's poem opens with the knight in a hostile environment where

> The sedge has withered from the lake,
> And no birds sing

while on his cheek 'a fading rose / Fast withereth too'. Keats beautifully transforms these various features of balladry into a unique poem that is worthy of its models.

Swinburne was an avid ballad collector and from 1858 planned reconstructions of traditional ballads as well as ballad imitations. Under the influence of Rossetti he began to write original poems in the ballad style, such as 'May Janet', 'The King's Daughter', 'The Brothers'. 'May Janet' is exceptionally successful. It tells of a father's opposition to a captain's love for his daughter; when the father decides to drown the unfortunate girl Swinburne demonstrates the imitative expertise which has allowed him to seize on stereotypical effects:

> Her father's drawn her by both hands,
> He's rent her gown from her,
> He's ta'en the smock round her body,
> Cast in the sea-water.

When Child's *English and Scottish Ballads* — a modest forerunner of his great collection — appeared in 1857-8 Swinburne abandoned the idea of publishing his own *Ballads of the English Border*.

Probably the most genuinely popular of the literary ballads came from the fecund mind of Rudyard Kipling. He had an unerring ear for the speech of the people and his ballads delighted a large audience. Many people still have them by heart. On 22 February 1890 the first Barrack-Room Ballad, 'Danny Deever', was included in W. E. Henley's weekly magazine the *Scots Observer*. In this poem Kipling brilliantly appropriated elements of the ballad style for his own purpose: the matter is presented in dialogue, the action is catastrophic, and there are commonplace items like the echoic phrasing of balladry ('so white, so white'). At the climax of the poem is a powerful yet seemingly artless image:

'What's that so black again the sun?' said Files-on-Parade.
'It's Danny fightin' 'ard for life', the Colour-Sergeant
said.

> 'What's that that whimpers over'ead?' said Files-on-
> Parade.
> 'It's Danny's soul that's passin' now', the Colour-
> Sergeant said.

After the first success the *Scots Observer* printed other major Kipling ballads during 1890, and in April 1892 Kipling published the first collected edition of *Barrack-Room Ballads:* it was reprinted three times that year and fifty times during the following thirty years. If not absorbed by 'the folk', it was accepted by many folk. Kipling was enchanted by balladry; in 1893 he produced 'The Last Rhyme of True Thomas' which has the prophetic poet rejecting a flattering offer from a king. It has details derived from such ballads as 'Sir Patrick Spens' (58) — 'And the first least word the proud King heard, / It harpit the salt tear out o' his e'e' — and displays Kipling's sheer technical skill. In his introduction to *A Choice of Kipling's Verse* (1941) T. S. Eliot thought that 'What is unusual about Kipling's ballads is his singleness of intention in attempting to convey no more to the simple minded than can be taken in on one reading or hearing'. That condescending reference to simplicity has its roots in Addison's original critique of balladry.

A. E. Housman, the pedantically combative Professor of Latin at University College, London, relied almost exclusively on the ballad stanza in his *A Shropshire Lad* (1896). On the one hand Housman was a scrupulous editor of classical texts; on the other he was a poet with profound Romantic tendencies. His use of the ballad stanza is poignant as well as metrically tight, and he added to the quatrain an aphoristic brevity, a moral concern:

> There sleeps in Shrewsbury jail to-night.
> Or wakes, as may betide,
> A better lad, if things went right,
> Than most that sleep outside.

It is not surprising that such lines made a great impact on Oscar Wilde who, in 1895, was sentenced to two years' imprisonment with hard labour for the sin of being himself in a hypocritical society. During his imprisonment Wilde, the dandy with an exquisite command of the English language, was to experience the extremes of humiliation. In November 1895, during his transfer from Wandsworth to Reading Gaol, he had to stand handcuffed before a jeering crowd at Clapham Junction. The following summer a young trooper was brought to Reading Gaol to face execution for the murder of his wife. After his release from prison Wilde published his 'Ballad of Reading Gaol' (1898); to express his new emotional depths Wilde reached for the ballad style. With its dignity and majestic movement this literary ballad was able to bring some realism back to Victorian literature. Wilde added two lines to the ballad stanza, and his sextet rhymed abcbdb. It represented something altogether new in his work and is easily his greatest poem:

> He did not wear his scarlet coat,
> For blood and wine are red,
> And blood and wine were on his hands,
> When they found him with the dead,
> The poor dead woman whom he loved,
> And murdered in her bed.

In 'Modern Poetry', a broadcast of 1936, W. B. Yeats remembered:

> My generation, because it disliked Victorian rhetorical moral fervour, came to dislike all rhetoric. . . . People began to imitate old ballads because an old ballad is never rhetorical. I think of A Shropshire Lad, of certain poems by Hardy, of Kipling's Saint Helena Lullaby, and his The Looking-Glass.

Like Keats, Yeats introduced a note of ambiguity into his ballads. 'The Host of the Air' from *The Wind Among the Reeds*

(1899) wraps a dreamlike atmosphere round a tale of bride-stealing:

> But he heard high up in the air
> A piper piping away,
> And never was piping so sad,
> And never was piping so gay.

Erza Pound, whose genius and inspirational example helped form the literary taste of the twentieth century, was convinced that ballads were created by individuals; poets of a previous age very much like himself. In a letter of 1 January 1918 to Harriet Monroe he said: 'The blessing of the "folk" song is solely in that the "folk" forget and leave out things. It is a fading and attrition not a creative process.' One of Pound's earliest successes was a 'Ballad of the Goodly Fere' in which Christ is portrayed not as the passive figure of religious piety but as a heroic activist. Pound constantly preached the necessity of poetic expertise and there is a typical virtuoso touch in his ballad: the b rhyme in the abcb quatrain is the same throughout the poem. Christ emerges larger than life in this ballad which is supposed to be spoken by Simon Zelotes 'somewhile after the Crucifixion'. The tone is well conveyed in this confident quatrain:

> A master of men was the Goodly Fere,
> A mate of the wind and sea,
> If they think they ha' slain our Goodly Fere
> They are fools eternally.

Hugh MacDiarmid's vernacular masterpiece, *A Drunk Man Lloks at the Thistle*, includes what I consider to be the most successful ballad imitation since Keats's 'La Belle Dame Sans Merci'; I refer to the six quatrain section often anthologized under the title 'O Wha's the Bride'. MacDiarmid was a Borderer — born in Langholm in 1892 — and he saw as his poetic mission in life the revival of Scots as a valid literary medium. To an astonishing degree he succeeded in setting the heather on fire through his one-man renaissance. His ballad 'O Wha's the Bride' reveals his poetic genius to perfection. Like the traditional ballad it plunges immediately into the tense situation with the unvirginal bride and the unsuspecting husband:

> O wha's the bride that cairries the bunch
> O' thistles blinterin' white?
> Her cuckold bridegroom little dreids
> What he sall ken this nicht.

That has the genuine ring of a popular idiom, an apparently effortless use of colloquial language to create an explosive situation. From that opening the poem develops into a mystical dialogue; for, in response to the husband's question 'O wha's been here afore me, lass / And hoo did he get in?', the bride explains that it was a man who died before she was born. However, she promises he will forget this intrusion on his sexual privacy in her beauty:

> *And on my lips ye'll heed nae mair,*
> *And in my hair forget,*
> *The seed o' a' the men that in*
> *My virgin womb ha'e met ...*

It is certain that the traditional ballad will continue to have a seminal influence on literature; there is hardly a writer of note who has not been drawn to the ballad. Examples could be multiplied to take in W. H. Auden's psychological ballads, like 'Miss Gee' and 'Victor', or the idiosyncratic use of the ballad idiom in Dylan Thomas's 'Ballad of the Long-Legged Bait' which uses enjambement (unlike the traditional ballads) but employs ballad-like epithets as in 'whale-blue eyes'. Charles Causley, too, has written a large number of literary ballads. But the influence of balladry is not confined to poetic imitations. In a splendid story, 'Sealskin Trousers', Eric Linklater considered the possibility that the selkie — from 'The Great Silkie of Sule Skerry' (113) — might represent a giant evolutionary leap for mankind. The same ballad inspired George Mackay Brown's story 'Sealskin'. Another Mackay Brown story, 'The Ballad of the Rose Bush', uses ballad logic to make its narrative point. It tells how a dumb girl, Margaret, is found bleeding at a well and how the guilty party is assumed to be Mick the tinker who is then hanged. Margaret dies embroidering a briar with a red rose in the heart of it and a rose bush grows out of Mick's grave. This can only mean, to those who know the rose-and-briar finale, that Margaret and Mick were true lovers and that he was innocent of the crime for which he was hanged. In ways such as this the ballads continue to stimulate literary invention.

The sharpest criticism aimed at the vulnerable body of contemporary poetry points out its remoteness from life. Artistic isolationism has proved a self-defeating policy; the poet of today is in danger of becoming only a law unto himself, solipsistically insisting he has no responsibility to anything but his own imagination. This supposed victory for creative privacy has left the poet in the position of a distracted actor roaring out his lines to an empty auditorium. If a substantial proportion of people are to listen to poetry again I suspect they will wish to listen to poetry that is about something and is formally and thematically rewarding. In this situation the ballad might come into its own again — not as a voice from the past but as a formal precedent capable of endless renewal.

Bibliography

The definitive collection of ballad texts is Francis James Child's *The English and Scottish Popular Ballads*, 5 vols (Boston, 1882-98; reprinted New York, 1965). What Child's major work of scholarship neglected was the musical dimension of balladry, and this has been supplied by Bertrand Harris Bronson's *The Traditional Tunes of the Child Ballads*, 4 vols (Princeton, NJ, 1959-72). Child and Bronson are the Gilbert and Sullivan of balladry: they have provided the words and music of a great popular idiom. What follows is a selection from the enormous literature relating to the ballads.

Bronson, Bertrand Harris, *Joseph Ritson: Scholar-at Arms*, 2 vols, Berkeley, 1938.

A fascinating biography of the man whose immense critical energy was spent on insisting that Percy's *Reliques* contained an abuse of editorial privilege and who insisted on an untampered presentation of ballad texts.

Bronson, Bertrand Harris, *The Ballad as Song*, Berkeley and Los Angeles, 1969.

A collection of essays and reviews reflecting the author's interest in the interdependence of tunes and texts.

Buchan, David, *The Ballad and the Folk*, London and Boston, 1972.

Confining himself to the north-east of Scotland — of which he is a native — the author examines the ballad as an oral phenomenon which atrophied with the advent of literacy; the most original aspect is the discussion of the architectonic structure of the ballads.

Buchan, David, (ed.), *A Scottish Ballad Book*, London and Boston, 1973.

Designed as a companion to the above, this anthology presents three stages of ballad transmission in Scotland's northeast: the oral ballads of Mrs Brown; the transitional ballads of James Nicol; bothy ballads and learned-by-rote ballads of Bell Robertson.

Chappell, William, *Popular Music of the Olden Time*, London, 1858.

Valuable collection of tunes from printed and manuscript sources.

Chappell, William, and Ebsworth, J. W. (eds), *Roxburghe Ballads*, 9 vols, Hertford and London, 1871-99.

This collection of more than 1300 (mainly blackletter) broadside ballads came into the hands of John, Duke of Roxburghe, in 1788; Child thought this and the Pepys broadside collection were, in the main, 'veritable dung-hills' (letter of 25 August 1872 to Grundtvig).

Collison, Robert, *The Story of Street Literature*, London, 1973.

More an annotated anthology than a history, this book quotes a mass of material from the Catnach Press and shows the connection between street literature and popular journalism.

Fowler, David C., *A Literary History of the Popular Ballad*, Durham, NC, 1968.

Discusses the connection between medieval romance and the decline of the minstrelsy in the fifteenth century and maintains (p. 18) that 'the English and Scottish ballads originated in the fifteenth century when the metrical romance tradition of the later Middle Ages joined the mainstream of folksong to create a type of narrative song which we now call the ballad'.

Friedman, Albert B., *The Ballad Revival*, Chicago, 1961.

'What we call the ballad revival ... was simply the translation of the genre from an active life on the popular level to a "museum life" on the sophisticated level,' says Friedman, who also takes Hustvedt and others to task for ignoring the similarities between the popular and the broadside ballad.

Friedman, Albert B. (ed.), *The Viking Book of Folk Ballads*, New York, 1956.

Substantial one-volume anthology including Irish, Australian, Canadian and American ballads as well as many from the Child canon; the thematic arrangement is admirable.

Gerould, Gordon Hall, *The Ballad of Tradition*, Oxford, 1932.

One of the finest critical books on the ballad, covering all aspects of the subject, and giving (p. 11) his now classic definition: 'A ballad is a folk-song that tells a story with stress on the crucial situation, tells it by letting the action unfold itself in event and speech, and tells it objectively with little comment or intrusion of personal bias.'

Graves, Robert (ed.), *The English Ballad*, London, 1927.

An anthology designed to illustrate the author's communalist thesis.

Greig, Gavin, *Last Leaves of Traditional Ballads and Ballad Airs*, Aberdeen, 1925.

This important collection (edited by Alexander Keith) contains 107 variants of Child ballads, collected from the recitation of Bell Robertson and others; it showed the survival of the idiom in the north-east of Scotland.

Grigson, Geoffrey (ed.), *The Penguin Book of Ballads*, Harmondsworth, 1975.

A selection from the whole range of balladry — from the Child canon to modern ballad imitations.

Gummere, F. B., *The Popular Ballad*, Boston, 1907.

Although Gummere's identification with the communalist cause has somewhat tarnished his image, this book shows the depth of his incidental insights.

Hales, J. W., and Furnivall, F. J. (eds), *Bishop Percy's Folio Manuscript*, 3 vols, London, 1867-8.

Child encouraged this project so he could have access to the material untouched by Percy's 'improving' hand; it revealed how little Percy had taken from his famous manuscript when preparing the *Reliques*.

Henderson, T. G., *The Ballad in Literature*, Cambridge, 1912.
The author's opposition to the communalists led him to argue that each ballad had a definite author and that the folk were more likely to ruin than re-create a ballad in the process of oral transmission.

Herd, David (ed.), *Ancient and Modern Scottish Songs*, 2 vols, Edinburgh, 1776.
An early anthology that displays editorial integrity in the presentation of ballad texts.

Hodgart, Matthew, *The Ballads*, London, 1950.
A short informative introduction to the subject.

Hodgart, Matthew (ed.), *The Faber Book of Ballads*, London, 1965.
Contains broadsides, Irish, Australian and American ballads as well as Child ballads.

Hustvedt, Sigurd Bernhard, *Ballad Books and Ballad Men*, Cambridge, Mass., 1930.
A survey of ballad collections since 1800, it stresses the influence of Denmark's Sven Grundtvig on Child; an important appendix contains the Grundtvig-Child correspondence of 1872-83.

Kinsley, James (ed.), *The Oxford Book of Ballads*, Oxford, 1969.
Replaces Sir Arthur Quiller-Couch's Oxford Book of 1910 with a greater regard for street and literary ballads.

Kittredge, George L., and Child Sargent, Helen (eds), *English and Scottish Popular Ballads*, Boston and New York, 1905.
A one-volume reduction of Child's collection; Kittredge's introduction is a trenchant statement of the communalist case.

Lang, Andrew, *Sir Walter Scott and the Border Minstrelsy*, London, 1910.
Defends Scott against the charge of fabricating ballads, spe-

cifically 'Auld Maitland' which, says Lang, Scott got 'from Hogg, who got it from recitation' (p. v).

Leach, MacEdward (ed.), *The Ballad Book*, New York and London, 1955.

Substantial anthology containing American ballads as well as 185 Child ballads.

Lloyd, A. L., *Folk Song in England*, London, 1967. Paperback ed. London, 1975.

A natural successor to Sharp as enthusiast of folksong, Lloyd gives a stimulating and radical account of industrial songs and sea shanties as well as what he calls 'The Big Ballads'.

Motherwell, William (ed.), *Minstrelsy Ancient and Modern*, Glasgow, 1827.

Motherwell's scrupulously scholarly approach to ballad texts influenced the editorial practice of Child's Danish mentor Sven Grundtvig, whose *Danmarks gamle Folkeviser* provided the plan for *The English and Scottish Popular Ballads*.

Muir, Willa, *Living With Ballads*, London, 1965.

Details the author's personal discovery of the world of balladry and folklore.

Palmer, Roy (ed.), *A Touch on the Times*, Harmondsworth, 1974.

An anthology — containing folksongs and fifty-two broadside ballads — covering the period 1770-1914.

Percy, Thomas, (ed.), *Reliques of Ancient English Poetry*, London, 1765.

Taking editorial liberties with his folio manuscript, Percy gave popular ballads literary respectability with the publication of this book.

Pinto, V. de Sola, and Rodway, A. E. (eds), *The Common Muse*, London, 1957.

An anthology of street balladry from the fifteenth to the twentieth centuries.

Pound, Louise, *Poetic Origins and the Ballad*, New York, 1921.

A detailed dismissal of the communalist case.

Reed, James, *The Border Ballads*, London, 1973.

Studies the Border ballads in their environmental and historical context.

Ritson, Joseph (ed.), *Robin Hood*, London, 1795.

The scourge of Percy and Pinkerton pioneered the modern method of presenting the ballads without editorial 'improvements'; this is one of his most enjoyable collections.

Rollins, Hyder E. (ed.), *The Pepys Ballads (1552-1702)*, 8 vols, Cambridge, Mass., 1929-32.

Annotated reprint of the Pepys collection of 1671 broadside ballads.

Scott, Walter, *Minstrelsy of the Scottish Border*, 3 vols, Kelso and Edinburgh, 1802-3.

Scott's editorial intention was 'to imitate the plan and style of Bishop Percy, observing only more strict fidelity concerning my originals'; his hugely enthusiastic approach to the subject put the Scottish Border prominently on the international artistic map.

Sharp, Cecil J., *English Folk Song: Some Conclusions*, London, 1907. 4th ed. 1965.

Written after four years of collecting folk tunes in Somerset, this book was a pugnacious and successful attempt to promote a folksong revival; Sharp's account of the evolution of the folksong has been generally accepted; this short book remains a classic of its kind.

Shepard, Leslie, *The Broadside Ballad*, London, 1962.

An enthusiast's view of street literature as the progenitor of the popular press.

Shepard, Leslie, *The History of Street Literature*, Newton Abbot, 1973.

Superbly illustrated account of street literature and its impact on popular culture.

Index of ballad titles

Index of names